PENGUIN CLASSICS

ECCE HOMO

FRIEDRICH NIETZSCHE was born near Leipzig in 1844, the son of a Lutheran clergyman. He attended the famous Pforta School, then went to university at Bonn and at Leipzig, where he studied philology and read Schopenhauer. When he was only 24 he was appointed to the chair of classical philology at Basle University; he stayed there until his health forced him into retirement in 1879. While at Basle he made and broke his friendship with Wagner, participated as an ambulance orderly in the Franco-Prussian War, and published *The Birth of Tragedy* (1872), *Untimely Meditations* (1873–6) and the first two parts of *Human, All Too Human* (1878–9). From 1880 until his final collapse in 1889, except for brief interludes, he divorced himself from everyday life and, supported by his university pension, he lived mainly in France, Italy and Switzerland. The third part of *Human, All Too Human* appeared in 1880, followed by *The Dawn* in 1881. *Thus Spoke Zarathustra* was written between 1883 and 1885, and his last completed books were *Ecce Homo*, an autobiography, and *Nietzsche contra Wagner*. He became insane in 1889 and remained in a condition of mental and physical paralysis until his death in 1900.

R. J. HOLLINGDALE has translated eleven of Nietzsche's books and published two books about him. He has also translated works by, among others, Schopenhauer, Goethe, E. T. A. Hoffmann, Lichtenberg and Theodor Fontane, many of these for the Penguin Classics. He is Honorary President of the British Nietzsche Society, and was for the Australian academic year 1991 Visiting Fellow at Trinity College, Melbourne.

MICHAEL TANNER was educated in the RAF and at Cambridge University, where he is a Lecturer in Philosophy and Dean of Corpus Christi College. He is equally interested in philosophy, music and literature, his particular areas being Nietzsche and Richard Wagner. He has written for many journals and contributed 'The Total Work of Art' to *The Wagner Companion*.

FRIEDRICH NIETZSCHE

ECCE HOMO

HOW ONE BECOMES
WHAT ONE IS

TRANSLATED WITH NOTES BY
R. J. Hollingdale

INTRODUCTION BY
Michael Tanner

PENGUIN BOOKS

PENGUIN BOOKS

Published by the Penguin Group
Penguin Books Ltd, 27 Wrights Lane, London W8 5TZ, England
Penguin Books USA Inc., 375 Hudson Street, New York, New York 10014, USA
Penguin Books Australia Ltd, Ringwood, Victoria, Australia
Penguin Books Canada Ltd, 10 Alcorn Avenue, Toronto, Ontario, Canada M4V 3B2
Penguin Books (NZ) Ltd, 182–190 Wairau Road, Auckland 10, New Zealand

Penguin Books Ltd, Registered Offices: Harmondsworth, Middlesex, England

This translation first published 1979
Reprinted with a new introduction 1992
3 5 7 9 10 8 6 4 2

Translation copyright © R. J. Hollingdale, 1979
New introduction copyright © Michael Tanner, 1992
All rights reserved

Typeset by Datix International Ltd, Bungay, Suffolk
Set in Monotype Garamond
Printed in England by Clays Ltd, St Ives plc

CONTENTS

INTRODUCTION

Ecce Homo is the title of Friedrich Nietzsche's autobiography. Almost certainly it is the most bizarre example of that genre ever penned. Its oddness begins with the title, which is a clear reference to St John's Gospel, where it is narrated that Pilate brought Jesus out with his crown of thorns for the Jews to see, and said to them: 'Behold the man!' So Nietzsche is evidently comparing himself to Christ, and whether seriously or in jest, the comparison remains equally blasphemous. But the subtitle is bewildering, and in a peculiarly Nietzschean way: one needs to read the whole book to see what it means and then to read Nietzsche's other books to see what it *really* means.

'How one becomes what one is.' Immediately several questions spring to the reader's mind. For instance: how could one fail to be what one is in the first place? So how can it make sense to say that one becomes what one is? And supposing that is what happens, can Nietzsche really tell us how it comes about, as his subtitle promises? And why '*what* one is'? Is it significant, as one uneasily feels it must be, that Nietzsche says 'what' rather than the more expectable 'who'? Thus in a state possibly of outrage and certainly of puzzlement, one moves on to the contents page where more surprises are waiting: the first three chapters are called 'Why I am So Wise', 'Why I am So Clever' and 'Why I Write Such Good Books'; the remainder are the titles of almost all of Nietzsche's books, except for the last chapter, 'Why I am a Destiny'.

Either, one suspects, this is a joke of a rather heavy-handed 'Teutonic' variety, or Nietzsche's madness, which is usually thought to have begun pretty abruptly early in January 1889, was actually under way while he was writing this book during the autumn of 1888. Neither of these suspicions is without foundation, but there is more to it than that. Though Nietzsche had no idea that this was to be his last book, indeed was full of plans for further ones, he seems to have felt that a point had been reached in his life and his work where a retrospective celebration was in place. By this time in his writing he was more fascinated than he had ever been by the possibilities of parody, and the traditional form of autobiography must have been enormously attractive. For what are autobiographies, in general, but prolonged celebrations of the achievements of their authors? The very idea of writing one's autobiography could be said to be megalomaniac; one is assuming that one's life is either sufficiently exemplary or sufficiently idiosyncratic to be worth retailing for general consumption. The lack of explicit self-congratulation that is one of the conventions of the form is merely a device for getting readers to note how modesty, too, is a quality the author has, besides all the others that emerge from his accounts of his actions and sufferings.

It isn't in the least surprising, then, that once Nietzsche had realized that the genre could so readily be adapted with mischievous intent, he should embark on it. And his mood during that whole year tended to be euphoric. It is a mistake to claim, as commentators often do, that it was an exceptionally prolific year; by Nietzsche's standards it wasn't. If one counts the titles of the books he wrote, or in two cases self-cannibalized, during 1888, the tally is indeed startling: *The Case of Wagner*, *Twilight of the Idols*, *The Antichrist*, *Dithyrambs of Dionysos*, *Nietzsche contra Wagner* and *Ecce Homo* itself. But none of them is very long, three in fact are of moderate pamphlet-length and all of them together are shorter than, say, *The Gay Science* or *Thus Spoke Zarathustra*. But they are all characterized by an intensity remarkable even for him, and usually, too (*The Antichrist* is the exception), by almost unrestrained ebullience. Extravagant in mode as they are, their extravagance is frequently of a parodic variety. The brevity with which Nietzsche performs only adds to the effect of laughing seriousness – something that Nietzsche had very often preached, but never before succeeded in practising so continuously and with so little sense of strain.

In one of his most famous passages, 'How the "Real World" at last Became a Myth' in *Twilight of the Idols*, he manages to produce a history of Western philosophy which is both hilarious and unnervingly accurate. Nietzsche divides up the history of the concept of the 'real world' into six stages, characterizes each of them in a couple of lines and then adds a parenthesized ironic commentary on the progress of the idea. Not only that, but the whole section is integrated into his own philosophy, so that as the 'real world' disappears Zarathustra makes his debut. But marvellous as that section is, the whole ninety pages of *Twilight of the Idols* is on the highest level, an amazing condensation of his mature views, and one of the most exhilarating intellectual and literary achievements I know of. The state of inspiration which he claims, in *Ecce Homo*, to have been in whilst writing *Thus Spoke Zarathustra* is far more plausibly attributable to him, in my view, during this last year of his sane life. And by the time he began to write *Ecce Homo*, he seems to have realized that some peak had been reached. For along with the high spirits, the manic self-celebrations, the parodistic orgies, there is a tone of elegy which consorts extraordinarily well with those other tones, producing an effect of a kind that is uniquely moving, especially when one knows that total and permanent breakdown was imminent.

The Foreword strikes a sombre, portentous note, of a kind familiar from many of Nietzsche's writings when he is concerned with the complete neglect that he suffered from his contemporaries, especially in his own country. The idea is given out here, and recurs as a leitmotif throughout the book, that the world is owed a reckoning by Nietzsche, since the effect he is about to have on it will be so cataclysmic that we must know what, and/or who, has hit us. While there can be no doubt that this claim of Nietzsche's is partly pathological – that he truly thought that he was about to achieve something earth-shattering – it also makes perfectly good sense insofar as the challenge that he presents us with, if we take it seriously, must radically alter our lives. And because, at this stage in his work, he identifies himself with the books he has written – or at least does that for some of the time – he feels that it is imperative that we understand him, if only so that we shall not confuse him with other life-changers who want us to know what they are like so that we can be like that too. Hence the cardinal significance of the closing words of the Foreword, quoted from *Thus Spoke Zarathustra*: 'You had not yet sought yourselves when you found me. Thus do all believers; therefore all belief is of so little account. Now I bid you lose me and find yourselves; and only *when you have all denied me* will I return to you . . .' This is perhaps Nietzsche's most succinct statement of his revulsion at the idea of living one's life by modelling it on what someone else said or did. One becomes what one is by not being anyone else – something that is in any case impossible, but that has not deterred most people, including all admirers of Thomas à Kempis's *Imitation of Christ*, a book for which Nietzsche felt especial distaste, from making the attempt.

If we take this as the major theme of *Ecce Homo*, a lot that seems absurd, exaggerated or merely false becomes, at the very least, highly interesting. For the book becomes an attempt to demonstrate, in a variety of more or less shocking ways, how Nietzsche contrived to achieve an independence of spirit in the face of a series of strong temptations to capitulate to powerful influences. Above all it tries to show how he practised a kind of systematic ingratitude towards those great figures who meant most to him, and how this is the only way of taking them completely seriously – whereas the usual view is that to take someone seriously is to allow them to dominate one to a degree that involves abandoning oneself, if only for a time. What commands admiration even in the shrillest passages of *Ecce Homo*, as in the other late works, is the candour with which Nietzsche exposes his own failings in this respect, while still turning them to positive account. How, in other words, does one turn discipleship into apostasy, while not betraying what one has been? As he puts it in the profound words of section 6 of the chapter on *Thus Spoke Zarathustra*, 'The psychological problem in the type of Zarathustra is how he, who to an unheard-of degree says No, *does* No to everything to which one has hitherto said Yes, can none the less be the opposite of a spirit of denial.' It isn't surprising that he doesn't give a straightforward answer to that question, but proceeds by considering the major figures in his development, figures who are, as always, personifications of attitudes to life which Nietzsche–Zarathustra (the predominance of Zarathustra in the book is partly the result of a degree of identification which Nietzsche had not previously allowed himself) has to take with all the seriousness due to his most dangerous opponents. Schopenhauer, Richard Wagner, Socrates, Christ make their final appearances – though the manner in which they do so shows that, if Nietzsche had continued to write, he would still have been preoccupied with them, since at least in the case of the last three, their seductiveness is something that one can never safely say one has conclusively overcome.

It is Richard Wagner to whom Nietzsche most obsessively returns in *Ecce Homo*, no doubt because he is the only major figure in Nietzsche's demonology with whom he had had a personal relationship, and one which Nietzsche was never inclined to devalue. The most lyrical passages of the book are expressions of what the relationship had meant, and therefore are all the more poignant because it had been essential to his spiritual well-being to terminate it. Section 5 of 'Why I am So Clever' is the most compressed statement in Nietzsche's work of the complexity of his feelings about Wagner:

I offer all my other human relationships cheap; but at no price would I relinquish from my life the Tribschen days, those days of mutual confidences, of cheerfulness, of sublime incidents − of *profound* moments ... I do not know what others may have experienced with Wagner: over *our* sky no cloud ever passed.

An idealization, no doubt, but it would be a steely soul who queried it. It makes all the more dramatic, of course, the rest of the section, where Wagner is shown to have become what he was not, and therefore to be the antipode of Nietzsche − though that is not how he puts it here; but that '[Wagner] became *reichsdeutsch*' is what Nietzsche says he couldn't forgive him. In other words, in this account, Wagner capitulated to the cultural pressures of the newly unified Germany, in all its loutish vulgarity, and allowed himself to be cast as its arch-representative in the arts.

But the dialectic of Wagner's inverted progress, and thus of Nietzsche's relationship to him, is more complicated than that. For the *delicatesse* which he is supposed to have renounced was a Parisian affair and thus already a matter of *décadence*, so that even before he became corrupted by the Reich, Wagner was of the tribe of Berlioz and Delacroix, who had 'a *fond* of sickness, of incurability in their nature, sheer fanatics for *expression*, virtuosi through and through ...' *Décadence* is, of course, one of the key terms in Nietzsche's later vocabulary, but the complexity of his feelings towards it is apparent both here, where he accuses Wagner of treachery towards it, and in the next section of the chapter, where he produces his most abandoned eulogy of Wagner the artist, in his ecstatic celebration of *Tristan und Isolde*:

I still today seek a work of a dangerous fascination, of a sweet and shuddery infinity equal to that of *Tristan* − I seek in all the arts in vain. All the strangenesses of Leonardo da Vinci lose their magic at the first note of *Tristan* ... The world is poor for him who has never been sick enough for this 'voluptuousness of hell'.

And more to the same effect.

Now, in a spectacular and altogether characteristic move, Nietzsche claims that it is the very dangerousness of *Tristan*, and the fact that he is able to incorporate it without being corrupted by it, that makes Wagner 'the great benefactor of my life'. Having one's cake and eating it could go no further. What is still more remarkable is that, in this context, the feat is justified. Nietzsche is here demonstrating how he was able to take something with a seriousness which is simply beyond the grasp of most people, and yet still not take it ultimately seriously, and so giving us a purchase on his much self-celebrated 'lightness', which elsewhere in his work can seem a sadly laboured affair. It is the high point in his work of that capacity for simultaneous celebration and critique which should exhilarate us as much as it obviously did him. And it is also the place where we can hope to grasp how the man who was so constant an exhorter to 'self-overcoming' should also have been the man who incited us to 'become ourselves'.

At Nietzsche's greatest moments he achieves an ecstasy which one would not have thought possible outside the context of a transcendental ideal in process of realization: the self, which we normally take as a given with which we have to live, making adjustments and modifications within fairly depressing limits, is revealed as something – or rather, less than something – capable of enormous expansion and transformation through the absorption of experiences which mostly we attempt to suppress or deny. And even worse than suppression and denial is regret. At this final stage of his life as a writer Nietzsche is so intent on regretting nothing that he moves to the opposite pole – but as he has so frequently reminded us in his later works, the 'faith in opposite values' is largely chimerical, so that we find, to our initial puzzlement, that there is a strong if not a pervasive tone of nostalgia, or something very like it, in these very last works. If it were nostalgia as we ordinarily think of it, Nietzsche would be performing a sleight of hand; for that kind of nostalgia is regret that the past is past. People are usually obsessed with the past, and in particular with their past, either because they wish it had been different or because they can't believe that things will ever again be so good. Nietzsche's concern with the past is a matter of delighting in its having been as it was, whatever that may have been, because it enables him to make the present so much better. Critical as he always was of the concept of redemption, he still writes in section 8 of the chapter on *Thus Spoke Zarathustra*: 'On one occasion Zarathustra strictly defines his task – it is also mine – the *meaning* of which cannot be misunderstood: he is *affirmative* to the point of justifying, of redeeming even the entire past.' And he goes on to quote one of the most celebrated but bewildering passages from that book, which concludes '*To redeem the past* and to transform every "It was" into an "I wanted it thus!" – that alone would I call redemption.'

For a long time I felt that that last exhortation of Zarathustra was only inspiring so long as one didn't enquire too carefully what it meant. For clearly the past cannot be changed and redemption would seem to require that. But what can be changed is our way of looking at it, of evaluating it. Even then, a great deal of anyone's life might seem irredeemable, in that it was time wasted, or put to futile or bad purposes. In other words, to eliminate the concept of regret from our outlook, to purge ourselves of nostalgia and remorse, demands a transformation of consciousness which we can hardly give sense to. But that is precisely Nietzsche–Zarathustra's point. The change he demands is one which, in depriving us of our humanity, would enable us to become superhuman. And 'there has never yet been a superman', Nietzsche tells us. Could there be, if this is the condition for its fulfilment? He is not concerned, in *Ecce Homo*, to answer that question. But what he does make vividly clear is the hopeless rut that we are all in if it can't be answered affirmatively.

It would be giving a grievously false impression of *Ecce Homo* to suggest that it is all on this solemn and imposing level. All told, it is Nietzsche's most mischievous book, in which along with self-celebrations which have led many readers to assume that he was already mad, there is an enormous amount of mockery, not least of the author. Often it isn't possible to say where mockery takes over; it is part of Nietzsche's 'most manifold art of style' that one is unsure which style he is practising. But at the same time another of the pairs of 'opposite values' that he routs in this book is that of seriousness and joking. For instance, there is no doubt that he means what he says in his stress on 'the little things' as being of an importance that philosophers have never granted them — climate, diet, digestion, when to read and so on. 'The whole casuistry of selfishness — . . . beyond all conception of greater importance than anything that has been considered of importance hitherto. It is precisely here that one has to begin to *learn anew* . . .' And he stresses that the organ he uses to come to his most important conclusions is his nose. 'I was the first to *discover* the truth, in that I was the first to sense — *smell* — the lie as lie . . . My genius is in my nostrils' ('Why I am a Destiny', 1). This passage follows almost immediately on his writing:

> I have a terrible fear I shall one day be pronounced *holy*: one will guess why I bring out this book *beforehand*; it is intended to prevent people from making mischief with me . . . I do not want to be a saint, rather even a buffoon . . . Perhaps I am a buffoon . . . and none the less, or rather *not* none the less — for there has hitherto been nothing more mendacious than saints — the truth speaks out of me.

Yet in the next section he writes:

> I am by far the most terrible human being there has ever been; this does not mean I shall not be the most beneficent.

His terrible fear that he would one day be pronounced holy came to pass at his funeral, when his friend, the composer Peter

Gast, said: 'May your name be holy to future generations' – a friend whom he praises extravagantly in the pages of *Ecce Homo*. The desperate jocularity of the book is justified; yet if it had been composed in uniformly serious tones it would have been no less misunderstood; no one knew better than Nietzsche that there is no insurance against stupidity. Therefore, it might be felt, he courted misunderstanding; the book has autobiographical passages which are easy to check up on and determine that they are false. It presents his life as if there had been a plan in it, which there evidently wasn't, and it alternates between the world-historical and the mundane in a way that was bound to offend its readers' taste, as it still does. But, Nietzsche would say, and almost does, so much the worse for their taste.

And it is in fact the very notion of taste, allied to that of smelling, which Nietzsche makes greatest and most inspired play with. In celebrating his capacity for locating decadence, for castigating the Germans for their deep-seated vulgarity, for revelling in destruction as a prerequisite of creation, for knowing what has to be created, Nietzsche is relying throughout on his extraordinarily developed sensitivity to phenomena which none of his contemporaries was able to notice, partly because they knew too much and esteemed the wrong kind of knowing. That is why he advertises his ignorance, his long-time refusal to read, which had earned him ostracism from the cultural community – the community of the 'philistines of culture', bogged down in their specializations, '*sick* with this inhuman clockwork and mechanism, with the *im*personality of the worker, with the false economy of "division of labour". The *goal* gets lost, culture – the means, the modern way of carrying on science, *barbarized*.' A great deal of *Ecce Homo* makes fun of the ghastliness of contemporary life, though time and again Nietzsche's almost boundless capacity for humour is overtaken by impatience at his fate in being ignored, and he is driven back to quoting *Thus Spoke Zarathustra* at its most portentous, even though 'to have understood, that is to say *experienced*, six sentences of that book would raise one to a higher level of mortals that "modern" man could attain to' ('Why I Write Such Good Books', 1). It is passages like that, and not the exuberantly auto-eulogistic ones, which are the most painful in the book. The tragedy of his life was that there were no means available to change people's taste, and without that he was bound to fail in his heroic endeavour, which lasted as long as he remained sane, and even for a few days after that, to make his contemporaries realize their plight. 'My time has not yet come, some are born posthumously,' he writes in the same paragraph as the previous quotation. And it is immediately followed by 'how *could* I, with *this* feeling of distance, even want the "modern men" I know – to read me!' but of course, that is what he did want, for their sake rather than his. If he could return now, he would find that 'modern men' are still what they were. They have still not understood that 'I have the right to understand myself as the first *tragic philosopher* – that is to say the extremest antithesis and antipodes of a pessimistic philosopher' ('The Birth of Tragedy', 3). And in answer to the final words of the book: '– Have I been understood? – *Dionysos against the Crucified . . .*' the answer must be a resounding 'No'.

Cambridge, April 1991   Michael Tanner

NOTE ON THE TEXT

THIS edition is annotated only lightly: its intention is to offer
the reader a clean, unobstructed text. Nietzsche wrote *Ecce
Homo* between 15 October and 4 November 1888 – that is to
say, in just under three weeks – but continued to make alterations and additions. In a letter to Overbeck dated 13 November
1888 he says that 'the manuscript of *Ecce Homo. How One
Becomes What One Is* is already with the printer'; subsequently he
asked the printer (Naumann, Leipzig) for the return of the
'second part of the manuscript' and then of the whole manuscript: it was sent back to him, but he kept it only two or three
days and returned it to Naumann on 6 December. Naumann
must have started setting the book at once, since by the date of
his breakdown Nietzsche had corrected the proofs of the title-
page, the list of contents, the Foreword, 'On this perfect day
. . .', the first chapter and the second chapter up to the words
'Caution, even hostility towards new books is rather part of my
instinct than "tolerance", "*largeur du coeur*" and other forms of
"neighbour love" . . .' in section 3. Up to this point no question
as to the validity of the text published in 1908 can arise, since
the author passed it for publication: it is over the remainder of
the text that controversy has arisen. It was started by Erich
Podach – a very experienced Nietzsche-scholar to whom a
Nietzsche-biographer is in debt – with the publication in 1961
of his *Friedrich Nietzsches Werke des Zusammenbruchs*, a printing
of manuscript versions of Nietzsche's last works with extensive
editorial comment. The item in which Podach's edition departs
most widely from the accepted version is *Ecce Homo*, which
Podach claims never achieved a final, completed form in

Nietzsche's hands, the accepted version being a redaction by Peter Gast: he then prints a version of *Ecce Homo* which includes variant passages, superseded drafts and repetitions. The violence of the criticism Erich Podach brought down upon himself for this edition was due, not to the publication of these variants in itself, but to the unpleasing acerbity of his own criticism of other editors and scholars and to his claim to have produced the only valid editions of the final works, a claim which was at once contested. The details of the controversy which ensued are too voluminous to be included here: its outcome, however, was in my judgement the vindication of the validity of *Ecce Homo* in its accepted form, with the proviso that some passages may have been suppressed (i.e. destroyed) and some repetitions eliminated when the original edition of 1908 was prepared. The strongest evidence that a final form was achieved by Nietzsche seems to me to be the fact that C. G. Naumann began setting the book in type – a thing he would hardly have done if he had not had a completed and legible MS before him. (The interested reader is referred for details of the controversy over Podach's edition firstly, of course, to the *Werke des Zusammenbruchs* itself, then to Walter Kaufmann's essay 'Nietzsche in the Light of his Suppressed Manuscripts', reprinted in the third edition of his *Nietzsche*; to Kaufmann's summary in the 'Note on the Publication of *Ecce Homo*' prefaced to his edition of *Ecce Homo*, in which he also translates and comments on variants from Nietzsche's drafts for the book; and to the 'Philologische Nachbericht' to Karl Schlechta's edition of Nietzsche's *Werke* and the 'Ergänzung' in the index volume to that edition.)

R. J. H.

CHRONOLOGY OF
NIETZSCHE'S LIFE

1844 Friedrich Wilhelm Nietzsche born (15 October) in the parsonage at Röcken, near Lützen, Prussian Saxony. His father, Karl Ludwig Nietzsche (*b*. 1813, the same year as Wagner), is the village pastor and the son of a pastor; his mother, Franziska Nietzsche (*b*. Oehler in 1826, and thus only eighteen years old), is the daughter of the pastor of the near-by village of Pobles. Friedrich Wilhelm – named after the reigning king of Prussia – is the first child of their marriage. They have two further children: Elizabeth (*b*. 10 July 1846) and Josef (*b*. February 1848, *d*. January 1850).

1849 Pastor Nietzsche dies (27 July): cause of death is given as 'softening of the brain' (encephalomalacia) following a fall.

1850 The family – now consisting of Nietzsche, his paternal grandmother, his mother, his sister and two maiden aunts – has to leave the parsonage and removes (April) to Naumburg, in Thuringia, where Nietzsche enters the town boys' school. In 1851 he transfers to a private preparatory school.

1854 He attends the high school (*Domgymnasium*), where he comes to be considered a gifted pupil. His surviving *juvenilia* confirm this judgement, although there is nothing to indicate precocious originality. During the summer of 1856 he is released from school because of persistent headaches and eye-trouble.

1858 The family moves to No. 18 Weingarten, subsequently the first 'Nietzsche Archive'. Nietzsche wins a free place at Schulpforta, the Prussian Rugby, and starts there on 5 October. At first he finds the discipline hard and suffers from homesickness: later, when he has discovered he has no difficulty in mastering the classical studies upon which the emphasis of the curriculum is laid and as a consequence comes to be regarded as an outstanding scholar, he enjoys being at Schulpforta. His attainments in other studies are, however, not remarkable. (The examining board are supposed on this account to have been on the point of refusing him the equivalent of a school-leaving certificate when one of them, presumably a classicist, exclaimed: 'But, *meine Herren*, are we really going to fail the best pupil Pforta has ever had?!')

1860 With two Naumburg friends, Wilhelm Pinder and Gustav Krug, he forms (25 July) a literary society, 'Germania', and for the following three years tries out essays, poems and compositions on the society. In March 1861 Krug lectures on *Tristan und Isolde*, and Nietzsche first hears Wagner. But his favourite composer throughout the Pforta years continues to be Schumann (*d.* 1856, but none the less a contemporary, 'modern' composer: the as yet unperformed *Tristan* is still the music of the future).

1864 He leaves Pforta (4 September) and enters Bonn University (16 October) as a student of theology and philology; in the latter subject he is a pupil of Friedrich Ritschl, whom he subsequently follows to Leipzig.

1865 Paul Deussen tells us (*Erinnerungen an Friedrich Nietzsche*) that Nietzsche tells him he has visited Cologne (February), where he has been taken to a brothel against his will, though he left again at once. As Nietzsche subsequently suffered from and eventually succumbed to syphilis, it seems probable that he does not leave at once or that he later returns. During 1867 he is treated by two Leipzig doctors for a syphilitic infection. (On Nietzsche's 'illness', and whether it was or was not syphilis: 1. As Nietzsche was a university student in the Germany of the 1860s to

1870s it would have been rather remarkable if he had *not* visited a brothel at least once. H. W. Brann, in his scholarly and entertaining study of Nietzsche's erotic life, *Nietzsche und die Frauen*, interprets the long poem which forms the staple of the chapter 'Among the Daughters of the Desert' in the fourth part of *Zarathustra* as a barely disguised recollection of a visit to a brothel – an interpretation which does not seem at all farfetched and originated in Brann's noticing similarities between its phraseology and that of Deussen's account mentioned above. [The poem, 'Die Wüste wächst', was also included by Nietzsche in the collection *Dionysos-Dithyramben*: that it is one of his worst does not affect its evidential value.] 2. The course of his illness from the first incapacitations in 1871 to total collapse at the beginning of 1889 is entirely typical of the disease in question – the only atypical aspect being the length of time between collapse and death [eleven years]. 3. As many passages in his writings, and especially some in the uninhibited *Ecce Homo*, disclose, Nietzsche was highly sexed, yet there is no record, or even hint, that he ever went to bed with a woman of his own class and, the documentation of his life being as ample as it is, we may conclude that he never did so. He had many women friends but not one wife or mistress. The reason may, as has very generally been assumed, be that he suffered from paralysing inhibition: but might this inhibition, if it really existed, not have originated in his knowledge that he suffered from something else too? something that, seeing he was a man of honour, must for ever keep him 'celibate' in relation to women of his own class? There are only two known occasions, recorded below, on which pressure of feeling overbore this restraint. [Richard Wagner believed he had discovered the cause of the young Nietzsche's frequent headaches and prostrations to lie in 'excessive masturbation', which diagnosis he communicated by letter to Nietzsche's doctor, Otto Eiser, of

Frankfurt: when he learned what Wagner had done, Nietzsche flew into a rage and declared he would never forgive what he termed 'this interference'.]) At Easter 1865 he abandons the study of theology (as a consequence of a loss of Christian belief) and on 17 August he leaves Bonn for Leipzig. At the end of October or beginning of November he buys a copy of Schopenhauer's *The World as Will and Idea* from a second-hand bookshop on an impulse, the book being then unknown to him: soon afterwards he announces to his friends that he has become a 'Schopenhaueran'.

1866 Nietzsche's work on Theognis convinces Ritschl Nietzsche is the most advanced pupil for his age he has ever taught and, on 24 February, he tells him so: thereafter Nietzsche is Ritschl's protégé. In the summer he reads F. A. Lange's *History of Materialism*. Beginning of his friendship with Erwin Rohde.

1867 Nietzsche's first publication: 'Zur Geschichte der Theognideischen Spruchsammlung' in the *Rheinische Museum für Philologie*. He is conscripted for a year's military service in the mounted section of a field artillery regiment (9 October–15 October 1868).

1868 'De Laertii Diogenis fontibus' and other philological studies published in the *Rheinische Museum* and *Litterarische Centralblatt* (also 1869). He is 'converted' to Wagner after a performance of the *Tristan* and *Meistersinger* preludes (28 October), and meets him for the first time eleven days later at the house of Wagner's brother-in-law Hermann Brockhaus: he learns that Wagner is also an admirer of Schopenhauer, and Wagner and Schopenhauer now combine to become what is emotionally Nietzsche's new religion.

1869 Nietzsche is appointed to the chair of classical philology at Basel and as teacher of Greek at the associated grammar school (13 February) at the age of twenty-four: he owes the appointment to Ritschl's recommendation. He is awarded his doctorate by Leipzig (23 March) without examination. At the request of Basel he applies to be relieved of his military obligations (i.e. to cease to be a citizen of Prussia) and for Swiss citizenship: the former application is granted; the latter is not, as he lacks the necessary residential qualification. (Nietzsche fails to renew this application and is consequently for the rest of his life stateless.) He arrives in Basel on 19 April. He visits Wagner at Tribschen, near Lucerne, on 15 May, is unable to see him and returns on 17 May; he is invited to attend Wagner's birthday celebrations on 22 May, but his teaching duties make this impossible. He pays his next visit for the weekend 5 to 7 June, and is thereafter a regular visitor: he stays with the Wagner family twenty-three times in the three years to April 1872, when Wagner leaves Tribschen for Bayreuth. Inaugural lecture on 'Homer and Classical Philology' delivered 28 May. He meets Jakob Burckhardt (*b.* 1818), the historian, and Franz Overbeck (*b.* 1837), the theologian. He spends Christmas with Wagner.

1870 Public lectures on 'The Greek Music-Drama' (18 January) and 'Socrates and Tragedy' (1 February). He obtains leave to serve as a medical orderly with the Prussian army (11 August): he collapses with dysentery and diphtheria (7 September) after tending casualties at Erlangen for three days and nights continuously. He returns to Basel at the end of October, and spends Christmas with Wagner, when he is present at the first performance of the *Siegfried Idyll* in the front hall at Tribschen.

1871 Nietzsche applies unsuccessfully for the chair of philosophy at Basel (January). He now begins to suffer from regularly recurring periods of exhaustion, and henceforward is never really well. On 15 February he is granted leave of absence 'for the purpose of restoring his health': he visits Lugano, the Bernese Oberland, Naumburg and Leipzig, and works on *The Birth of Tragedy*. He returns to Basel at the end of the year.

1872 *The Birth of Tragedy* published January. Public lectures 'On the Future of our Educational Institutions' (16 January, 6 and 27 February, 5 and 23 March). He attends the laying of the foundation stone of the Festival Theatre at Bayreuth (22 May). Meeting with Paul Rée.

1873 *Untimely Meditations I: David Strauss* published.

1874 *Untimely Meditations II: On the Use and Disadvantage of History*, and *III: Schopenhauer as Educator* published. During this year Nietzsche first becomes fully conscious of a previously unconscious dissatisfaction with and rebellion against Wagner–Schopenhauer, and thus begins consciously to resist and deny this dissatisfaction: the outcome is a state of internal tension which leads to such incidents as the violent scene between him and Wagner on the occasion of what was to prove his last private visit (August). After this visit he does not see Wagner again for nearly two years.

1875 Meeting with Peter Gast, afterwards his earliest 'disciple'. Violent headaches and vomiting attacks in June mean he cannot visit Bayreuth as intended: he goes for a 'cure' to Steinabad, in the Black Forest, and at once begins to feel much better. Elizabeth moves to Basel and sets up home for herself and her brother. Nietzsche suffers a general collapse at Christmas.

1876 He is granted a long period of absence from Basel because of his persistent ill-health. At Geneva he proposes marriage to one Mathilde Trampedach, and is rejected. In mid-April he returns to Basel. *Untimely Meditations IV: Richard Wagner in Bayreuth* published July. On 24 July he arrives in Bayreuth for the first festival, attends rehearsals, but is forced by the state of his head and eyes to leave before the festival proper begins: he goes to Klingenbrunn, in the Bavarian Forest, where he spends much of his time writing psychological reflections which will later be incorporated into *Human, All Too Human*. After ten days Elizabeth writes asking him to return to Bayreuth, which he does on 12 August and attends the first public cycle of *The Nibelung's Ring* (13, 14, 16 and 17 August). He avoids Wagner, fails to attend the second cycle, and on 27 August returns to Basel. The university grants him sick leave for a year (15 October): he has already left for Bex, Canton Waadt, and on 20 October he goes with Rée and the novelist Albert Brenner to Sorrento, where they stay with Malwida von Meysenburg at a villa she has rented on the coast with a view across the sea to Naples and Vesuvius. All three work on books, Rée on *The Origin of the Moral Sensations*, Nietzsche on *Human, All Too Human*. Wagner is also in Sorrento, and he and Nietzsche meet for the last time.

1877   He leaves Sorrento in May, travels alone in Italy and Switzerland, arrives back in Basel in the autumn: he sets up house again with Elizabeth, Gast making a third (1 September), and resumes teaching.

1878   *Human, All Too Human* published May. In June Elizabeth goes back to Naumburg. Wagner lets it be known he regards *Human* as evidence its author has suffered a mental breakdown: 'I have done him the kindness ... of *not* reading his book, and my greatest wish and hope is that one day he will thank me for this.' Other acquaintances were also estranged by the new book.

1879   *Assorted Opinions and Maxims* ('first supplement' to *Human, All Too Human*) published in February. In April Nietzsche suffers the worst and most protracted attack of migraine and sickness he has yet experienced: Overbeck wires Elizabeth, who comes to Basel and finds Nietzsche apparently on the point of death. On 2 May he petitions the university for release from all duties: on 14 June he is retired on a pension. He travels with Elizabeth to Schloss Bremgarten, near Bern, then to Zürich, then alone to St Moritz: there he completes *The Wanderer and his Shadow* ('second supplement' to *Human, All Too Human*) in September. In October he goes to Naumburg. He suffers severe attacks on 118 days of this year.

1880 *The Wanderer and his Shadow* published, *Daybreak* written. Nietzsche to Riva (February), where he is joined by Gast; to Gast's home in Venice (March); to Marienbad (June); back to Naumburg (September); then south again to Basel, Stresa, Genoa, where he spends the winter. His attitude towards his invalid condition is 'philosophical': 'The daily battle against headache and the laughable diversity of my ailments demands such an amount of attention that I am running into the danger of becoming *petty* – but this is a counterweight to those very ... high-flying tendencies that have such power over me that without some counterweight to them I would become a fool.'

1881 *Daybreak* published in June, *The Gay Science* begun. Nietzsche to Recoaro and Riva with Gast (April), and alone to St Moritz (June). Later in June to Sils-Maria – 'I know of nothing more suited to my nature than this piece of high land' – and takes up lodgings in a room attached to the house of the Bürgermeister. Back to Genoa in October. In November he sees *Carmen* for the first time and adopts it as the model antithesis to Wagner.

1882 *The Gay Science* completed in July and published in the autumn. Paul Rée with Nietzsche in Genoa (February), leaves for Rome in March, where at Malwida's house he meets Lou Salomé and proposes marriage to her. Nietzsche goes to Messina (end of March), then to Rome (end of April), where Rée introduces him to Lou. Two days afterwards Rée tells Lou Nietzsche has asked him to propose to her on his behalf. Lou declines to marry either man, and counterproposes a platonic *ménage-à-trois*: both, *faute de mieux*, agree. They all spend much time together, and are photographed in a photographer's mock-up of a cart, with Nietzsche and Rée between the shafts and Fräulein Salomé driving: Frl. Salomé is jocularly flourishing a whip. Lou Salomé, twenty-one, is the least strait-laced and most entertaining woman Nietzsche has yet met; also the most intelligent; and he falls in love with her. At Lucerne in May he proposes to her in person and is again rejected: Lou is a new-style liberated woman dedicated to independence. But the *ménage-à-trois* is still on, Vienna being the proposed venue. All this is kept secret from his mother and sister, as they would have considered it extremely immoral. Nietzsche, Lou and Elizabeth at Tautenburg (Thuringia) during August: Elizabeth becomes acquainted with the immoral plan and on the day Lou leaves (26 August) there is a scene between brother and sister. Nietzsche to Naumburg: Elizabeth writes to their mother telling her what is going on, and there is a scene between mother and son. Nietzsche to Leipzig: three weeks with Lou and Rée, who leave without arranging to meet him again; during the following month (November) it is borne in upon him that he has been abandoned. Nietzsche to Basel, to Genoa, to Rapallo: he is frantic with disappointment and self-contempt, and emotionally and physically almost exhausted.

1883 *Thus Spoke Zarathustra*, Part One, written in January–February: Nietzsche recovers his equilibrium by means of it. Wagner dies in Venice 13 February. Reconciliation with Elizabeth. Nietzsche to Genoa and Rome (May–June), to Sils-Maria (June), where he writes *Zarathustra*, Part Two. Both parts published. In September he returns to Naumburg, and learns Elizabeth is engaged to marry Bernhard Förster, a prominent anti-Semite. In October to Genoa, in November to Nice.

1884 *Zarathustra*, Part Three, written during January and published later in the year. Preparation of *The Will to Power* begun. Nietzsche to Venice (April) and Sils-Maria (July); in October to Zürich (meeting with Gottfried Keller), then back to Nice.

1885 *Zarathustra*, Part Four, written and privately printed. Nietzsche to Venice (April) and Sils-Maria (June). Elizabeth and Förster marry (22 May, the late Wagner's birthday), and leave for the colony of New Germania, in Paraguay. Nietzsche to Naumburg (September), then back to Nice (November).

1886 *Beyond Good and Evil* written and published. Nietzsche to Naumburg (May): last meeting with Rohde, in Leipzig. Back to Sils-Maria (July), then to Genoa (September) and Nice (October). Prefaces for new editions of his earlier works (and 1887).

1887 *On the Genealogy of Morals* written and published. Nietzsche to Sils-Maria (June), Venice (September), back to Nice (October).

1888 *The Wagner Case* written and published; *The Will to Power* abandoned, the *Revaluation of All Values* substituted, *Twilight of the Idols* written and prepared for publication; *The Anti-Christ* and *Ecce Homo* written; *Nietzsche contra Wagner* and the *Dithyrambs of Dionysos* assembled. Nietzsche to Turin (April), Sils-Maria (June), back to Turin (September). On 1 January the Bern *Bund* carries the first published review of his work as a whole (by Karl Spitteler); in April Georg Brandes lectures on his philosophy at Copenhagen. He experiences a delusive improvement in his health, and in the last quarter of the year is the victim of a morbid euphoria which is the immediate prelude to complete collapse.

1889 The *Revaluation of All Values* abandoned. Nietzsche collapses in the piazza Carlo Alberto, Turin (3 January): when he recovers consciousness he is no longer sane. He sends brief letters to friends, acquaintances and public figures announcing his arrival as 'Dionysos' or 'the Crucified'. Overbeck comes to Turin and takes Nietzsche to the university clinic at Basel (10 January). Diagnosis: 'paralysis progressiva'. On 17 January he is transferred to the university clinic at Jena. *Twilight of the Idols* published end of January, *Nietzsche contra Wagner* privately printed. Förster commits suicide in Paraguay (June) from fear of prosecution for frauds in connection with his colonial enterprise.

1890 Nietzsche's mother takes him back with her to No. 18 Weingarten, Naumburg, where he enters into her sole care.

1892 A collected edition of Nietzsche's published works and a selection from his notebooks is planned, with Gast as editor.

1893 Elizabeth returns from Paraguay, and Gast's edition is (1894) abandoned at her insistence ('who appointed *you* editor, then?'); she inaugurates a second collected edition, which is also subsequently abandoned because of disagreements over editorial methods. In February (1894) she founds the 'Nietzsche Archive' at No. 18 Weingarten.

1895 *The Anti-Christ* and *Nietzsche contra Wagner* published. Elizabeth becomes the owner of Nietzsche's copyright. Nietzsche, mentally a child, begins to become paralysed.

1896 Elizabeth moves the 'Archive' to Weimar.

1897 Nietzsche's mother dies (20 April): Elizabeth transfers him to Weimar and lodges him and the Archive in the Villa Silberblick.

1899 A third collected edition begun.

1900 Nietzsche dies in Weimar (25 August).

ECCE HOMO

HOW ONE BECOMES
WHAT ONE IS

FOREWORD

1

SEEING that I must shortly approach mankind with the heaviest demand that has ever been made on it, it seems to me indispensable to say *who I am*. This ought really to be known already: for I have not neglected to 'bear witness' about myself. But the disparity between the greatness of my task and the *smallness* of my contemporaries has found expression in the fact that I have been neither heard nor even so much as seen. I live on my own credit, it is perhaps merely a prejudice that I am alive at all? . . . I need only to talk with any of the 'cultured people' who come to the Ober-Engadin in the summer to convince myself that I am *not* alive . . . Under these circumstances there exists a duty against which my habit, even more the pride of my instincts revolts, namely to say: *Listen to me! for I am thus and thus. Do not, above all, confound me with what I am not!*

2

I am, for example, absolutely not a bogey-man, not a moral-monster – I am even an antithetical nature to the species of man hitherto honoured as virtuous. Between ourselves, it seems to me that precisely this constitutes part of my pride. I am a disciple of the philosopher Dionysos, I prefer to be even a satyr rather than a saint. But you have only to read this writing. Perhaps I have succeeded in giving expression to this antithesis in a cheerful and affable way – perhaps this writing had no point at all other than to do this. The last thing *I* would promise would be to 'improve' mankind. I erect no new idols;

let the old idols learn what it means to have legs of clay. *To overthrow idols* (my word for 'ideals') – that rather is my business. Reality has been deprived of its value, its meaning, its veracity to the same degree as an ideal world has been *fabricated* . . . The 'real world' and the 'apparent world' – in plain terms: the *fabricated* world and reality . . . The *lie* of the ideal has hitherto been the curse on reality, through it mankind itself has become mendacious and false down to its deepest instincts – to the point of worshipping the *inverse* values to those which alone could guarantee it prosperity, future, the exalted *right* to a future.

3

– He who knows how to breathe the air of my writings knows that it is an air of the heights, a *robust* air. One has to be made for it, otherwise there is no small danger one will catch cold. The ice is near, the solitude is terrible – but how peacefully all things lie in the light! how freely one breathes! how much one feels *beneath* one! – Philosophy, as I have hitherto understood and lived it, is a voluntary living in ice and high mountains – a seeking after everything strange and questionable in existence, all that has hitherto been excommunicated by morality. From the lengthy experience afforded by such a wandering in the *forbidden* I learned to view the origin of moralizing and idealizing very differently from what might be desirable: the *hidden* history of the philosophers, the psychology of their great names came to light for me. – How much truth can a spirit *bear*, how much truth can a spirit *dare*? that became for me more and more the real measure of value. Error (– belief in the ideal –) is not blindness, error is *cowardice* . . . Every acquisition, every step forward in knowledge is the *result* of courage, of severity towards oneself, of cleanliness with respect to oneself . . . I do not refute ideals, I merely draw on gloves in their presence . . . *Nitimur in* vetitum: in this sign my philosophy will one day conquer, for what has hitherto been forbidden on principle has never been anything but the truth. –

4

4

– Within my writings my *Zarathustra* stands by itself. I have with this book given mankind the greatest gift that has ever been given it. With a voice that speaks across millennia, it is not only the most exalted book that exists, the actual book of the air of the heights – the entire fact man lies at a tremendous distance *beneath* it – it is also the *profoundest*, born out of the innermost abundance of truth, an inexhaustible well into which no bucket descends without coming up filled with gold and goodness. Here there speaks no 'prophet', none of those gruesome hybrids of sickness and will to power called founders of religions. One has above all to *hear* correctly the tone that proceeds from this mouth, this halcyon tone, if one is not to do pitiable injustice to the meaning of its wisdom. 'It is the stillest words which bring the storm, thoughts that come on doves' feet guide the world –'

The figs are falling from the trees, they are fine and sweet: and as they fall their red skins split. I am a north wind to ripe figs.

Thus, like figs, do these teachings fall to you, my friends: now drink their juice and eat their sweet flesh! It is autumn all around and clear sky and afternoon –

Here there speaks no fanatic, here there is no 'preaching', here *faith* is not demanded: out of an infinite abundance of light and depth of happiness there falls drop after drop, word after word – a tender slowness of pace is the tempo of these discourses. Such things as this reach only the most select; it is an incomparable privilege to be a listener here; no one is free to have ears for Zarathustra ... With all this, is Zarathustra not a *seducer*? ... But what does he himself say when for the first time he again goes back into his solitude? Precisely the opposite of that which any sort of 'sage', 'saint', 'world-redeemer' and other *décadent* would say in such a case ... He does not only speak differently, he *is* different ...

I now go away alone, my disciples! You too now go away and be alone! So I will have it.

Go away from me and guard yourselves against Zarathustra! And better still: be ashamed of him! Perhaps he has deceived you.

The man of knowledge must be able not only to love his enemies but also to hate his friends.

One repays a teacher badly if one remains only a pupil. And why, then, should you not pluck at my laurels?

You respect me; but how if one day your respect should tumble? Take care that a falling statue does not strike you dead!

You say you believe in Zarathustra? But of what importance is Zarathustra? You are my believers: but of what importance are all believers?

You had not yet sought yourselves when you found me. Thus do all believers; therefore all belief is of so little account.

Now I bid you lose me and find yourselves; and only *when you have all denied me* will I return to you . . .

FRIEDRICH NIETZSCHE

On this perfect day, when everything has become ripe and not only the grapes are growing brown, a ray of sunlight has fallen on to my life: I looked behind me, I looked before me, never have I seen so many and such good things together. Not in vain have I buried my forty-fourth year today, I was *entitled* to bury it – what there was of life in it is rescued, is immortal. The first book of the *Revaluation of all Values*, the *Songs of Zarathustra*, the Twilight of the Idols, my attempt to philosophize with a hammer – all of them gifts of this year, of its last quarter even! *How should I not be grateful to my whole life?* – And so I tell myself my life.

WHY I AM SO WISE

I

THE fortunateness of my existence, its uniqueness perhaps, lies in its fatality: to express it in the form of a riddle, as my father I have already died, as my mother I still live and grow old. This twofold origin, as it were from the highest and the lowest rung of the ladder of life, at once *décadent* and *beginning* – this if anything explains that neutrality, that freedom from party in relation to the total problem of life which perhaps distinguishes me. I have a subtler sense for signs of ascent and decline than any man has ever had, I am the teacher *par excellence* in this matter – I know both, I am both. – My father died at the age of thirty-six: he was delicate, lovable and morbid, like a being destined to pay this world only a passing visit – a gracious reminder of life rather than life itself. In the same year in which his life declined mine too declined: in the thirty-sixth year of my life I arrived at the lowest point of my vitality – I still lived, but without being able to see three paces in front of me. At that time – it was 1879 – I relinquished my Basel professorship, lived through the summer like a shadow in St Moritz and the following winter, the most sunless of my life, *as* a shadow in Naumburg. This was my minimum: 'The Wanderer and his Shadow' came into existence during the course of it. I undoubtedly knew all about shadows in those days ... In the following winter, the first winter I spent in Genoa, that sweetening and spiritualization which is virtually inseparable from an extreme poverty of blood and muscle produced 'Daybreak'. The perfect brightness and cheerfulness, even exuberance of spirit reflected in the said work is in my case compatible not only with the profoundest physiological weakness, but even with an extremity of pain. In the midst of the torments which attended an uninterrupted three-day headache accompanied by the laborious vomiting of phlegm – I possessed a dialectical clarity *par excellence* and thought my way very cold-bloodedly through things for which when I am in better health I am not enough of a climber, not refined, not *cold* enough. My readers perhaps know the extent to which I regard dialectics as a symptom of *décadence*, for example in the most famous case of all: in the case of Socrates. – All morbid disturbances of the intellect, even that semi-stupefaction consequent on fever, have remained to this day totally unfamiliar things to me, on their nature and frequency I had first to instruct myself by scholarly methods. My blood flows slowly. No one has ever been able to diagnose fever in me. A doctor who treated me for some time as a nervous case said at last: 'No! there is nothing wrong with your nerves, it is only I who am nervous.' Any kind of local degeneration absolutely undemonstrable; no organically originating stomach ailment, though there does exist, as a consequence of general exhaustion, a profound weakness of the gastric system. Condition of the eyes, sometimes approaching dangerously close to blindness, also only consequence, not causal: so that with every increase in vitality eyesight has also again improved. – Convalescence means with me a long, all too long succession of years – it also unfortunately means relapse, deterioration, periods of a kind of *décadence*. After all this do I need to say that in questions of *décadence* I am *experienced*? I have spelled it out forwards and backwards. Even that filigree art of grasping and comprehending in general, that finger for nuances, that psychology of 'looking around the corner' and whatever else characterizes me was learned only then, is the actual gift of that time in which everything in me became more subtle, observation itself together with all the organs of observation. To look from a morbid perspective towards *healthier* concepts and values, and again conversely to look down from the abundance and certainty of *rich* life into the secret labour of the instinct of *décadence* – that is what I have practised most, it has been my own particular field of experience, in this if in anything I am a master. I now have the skill and knowledge to *invert perspectives*: first reason why a 'revaluation of values' is perhaps possible at all to me alone. –

2

Setting aside the fact that I am a *décadent*, I am also its antithesis. My proof of this is, among other things, that in combating my sick conditions I always instinctively chose the *right* means: while the *décadent* as such always chooses the means harmful to him. As *summa summarum* I was healthy, as corner, as speciality I was *décadent*. That energy for absolute isolation and detachment from my accustomed circumstances, the way I compelled myself no longer to let myself be cared for, served, *doctored* – this betrayed an unconditional certainty of instinct as to *what* at that time was needful above all else. I took myself in hand, I myself made myself healthy again: the precondition for this – every physiologist will admit it – is that *one is fundamentally healthy*. A being who is typically morbid cannot become healthy, still less can he make himself healthy; conversely, for one who is typically healthy being sick can even be an energetic *stimulant* to life, to more life. Thus in fact does that long period of sickness seem to me *now*: I discovered life as it were anew, myself included, I tasted all good and even petty things in a way that others could not easily taste them – I made out of my will to health, to *life*, my philosophy . . . For pay heed to this: it was in the years of my lowest vitality that I *ceased* to be a pessimist: the instinct for self-recovery *forbade* to me a philosophy of indigence and discouragement . . . And in what does one really recognize that someone has *turned out well*! In that a human being who has turned out well does our senses good: that he is carved out of wood at once hard, delicate and sweet-smelling. He has a taste only for what is beneficial to him; his pleasure, his joy ceases where the measure of what is beneficial is overstepped. He divines cures for injuries, he employs ill chances to his own advantage; what does not kill him makes him stronger. Out of everything he sees, hears, experiences he instinctively collects together *his* sum: he is a principle of selection, he rejects much. He is always in *his* company, whether he traffics with books, people or landscapes: he does honour when he *chooses*, when he *admits*, when he *trusts*. He reacts slowly to every kind of stimulus, with that slowness which a protracted caution and a willed pride have bred in him – he tests an approaching stimulus, he is far from going out to meet it. He believes in neither 'misfortune' nor in 'guilt': he knows how to *forget* – he is strong enough for everything to *have* to turn out for the best for him. Very well, I am the *opposite* of a *décadent*: for I have just described *myself*.

3

I consider the fact that I had such a father as a great privilege: the peasants he preached to – for, after he had lived for several years at the court of Altenburg, he was a preacher in his last years – said that the angels must look like he did. And with this I touch on the question of race. I am a pure-blooded Polish nobleman, in whom there is no drop of bad blood, least of all German. When I look for my profoundest opposite, the incalculable pettiness of the instincts, I always find my mother and my sister – to be related to such *canaille* would be a blasphemy against my divinity. The treatment I have received from my mother and my sister, up to the present moment, fills me with inexpressible horror: there is an absolutely hellish machine at work here, operating with infallible certainty at the precise moment when I am most vulnerable – at my highest moments ... for then one needs all one's strength to counter such a poisonous viper ... physiological contiguity renders such a *disharmonia praestabilita* possible ... But I confess that the deepest objection to the 'Eternal Recurrence', my real idea from the abyss, is always my mother and my sister. – But even as a Pole I am a monstrous atavism. One would have to go back centuries to find this noblest of races that the earth has ever possessed in so instinctively pristine a degree as I present it. I have, against everything that is today called *noblesse*, a sovereign feeling of distinction – I wouldn't award to the young German Kaiser the honour of being my coachman. There is one single case where I acknowledge my equal – I recognize it with profound gratitude. Frau Cosima Wagner is by far the noblest nature; and, so that I shouldn't say one word too few, I say that Richard Wagner was by far the most closely related man to me ... The rest is silence ... All the prevalent notions of degrees of kinship are physiological nonsense in an unsurpassablè measure. The Pope still deals today in this nonsense. One is least related to one's parents: it would be the most extreme sign of vulgarity to be related to one's parents. Higher natures have their origins infinitely farther back, and with them much had to be assembled, saved and hoarded. The great individuals are the oldest: I don't understand it, but Julius Caesar could be my father – or Alexander, this Dionysos incarnate ... At the very moment that I am writing this the post brings me a Dionysos-head.

4

I have never understood the art of arousing enmity towards myself – this too I owe to my incomparable father – even when it seemed to me very worthwhile to do so. However unchristian it may seem, I am not even inimical towards myself, one may turn my life this way and that, one will only rarely, at bottom only once, discover signs that anyone has borne ill will towards me – perhaps, however, somewhat too many signs of *good* will ... My experiences even of those of whom everyone has bad experiences speak without exception in their favour; I tame every bear, I even make buffoons mind their manners. During the seven years in which I taught Greek to the top form of the Basel grammar school I never once had occasion to mete out a punishment; the laziest were industrious when they were with me. I am always up to dealing with any chance event; I have to be unprepared if I am to be master of myself. Let the instrument be what it will, let it be as out of tune as only the instrument 'man' can become out of tune – I should have to be ill not to succeed in getting out of it something listenable. And how often have I heard from the 'instruments' themselves that they had never heard themselves sound so well . . . Most beautifully perhaps from that Heinrich von Stein who died so unpardonably young and who, after cautiously obtaining permission, once appeared for three days at Sils-Maria, explaining to everyone that he had *not* come for the Engadin. This excellent man, who with the whole impetuous artlessness of a Prussian Junker had waded into the Wagnerian swamp (– and into the swamp of Dühring in addition!), was during those three days as if transported by a storm-wind of freedom, like one suddenly raised to *his own* heights and given wings. I kept telling him it was the result of the fine air up here, that everyone felt the same, that you could not stand 6,000 feet above Bayreuth and not notice it – but he would not believe me . . . If, this notwithstanding, many great and petty misdeeds have been committed against me, it was not 'will', least of all *ill* will that was the cause of it: I could complain, rather – I have just suggested as much – of the good will which has caused me no little mischief in my life. My experiences give me a right to a general mistrust of the so-called 'selfless' drives, of the whole 'love of one's neighbour' which is always ready with deeds and advice. It counts with me as weakness, as a special case of the incapacity to withstand stimuli – it is only among *décadents* that *pity* is called a virtue. My reproach against those who practise pity is that shame, reverence, a delicate feeling for distance easily eludes them, that pity instantly smells of mob and is so like bad manners as to be mistaken for them – that the hands of pity can under certain circumstances intrude downright destructively into a great destiny, into a solitariness where wounds are nursed, into a *privilege* for great guilt. I count the overcoming of pity among the *noble* virtues: I have, as 'Zarathustra's Temptation', invented a case in which a great cry of distress reaches him, in which pity like an ultimate sin seeks to attack him, to seduce him from allegiance to *himself*. To remain master here, here to keep the *elevation* of one's task clean of the many lower and more shortsighted drives which are active in so-called selfless actions, that is the test, the final test perhaps, which a Zarathustra has to pass – the actual *proof* of his strength . . .

5

In yet another point I am merely my father once more and as it were the continuation of his life after an all too early death. Like anyone who has never lived among his equals and to whom the concept 'requital' is as inaccessible as is for instance the concept 'equal rights', I forbid myself in cases where a little or *very great* act of folly has been perpetrated against me any counter-measure, any protective measure – also, as is reasonable, any defence, any 'justification'. My kind of requital consists in sending after the piece of stupidity as quickly as possible a piece of sagacity: in that way one may perhaps overtake it. To speak in a metaphor: I dispatch a pot of jam to get rid of a *sour* affair . . . Let anyone harm me in any way, I 'requite' it, you may be sure of that: as soon as I can I find an opportunity of expressing my thanks to the 'offender' (occasionally even for the offence) – or of *asking* him for something, which can be more courteous than giving something . . . It also seems to me that the rudest word, the rudest letter are more good-natured, more honest than silence. Those who keep silent almost always lack subtlety and politeness of the heart; silence is an objection, swallowing down necessarily produces a bad character – it even ruins the stomach. All those given to silence are dyspeptic. – One will see that I would not like to see rudeness undervalued, it is the *most humane* form of contradiction by far and, in the midst of modern tendermindedness, one of our foremost virtues. – If one is rich enough, it is even fortunate to be in the wrong. A god come to earth ought to *do* nothing whatever but wrong: to take upon oneself, not the punishment, but the *guilt* – only that would be godlike.

6

Freedom from *ressentiment*, enlightenment over *ressentiment* – who knows the extent to which I ultimately owe thanks to my protracted sickness for this too! The problem is not exactly simple: one has to have experienced it from a state of strength and a state of weakness. If anything whatever has to be admitted against being sick, being weak, it is that in these conditions the actual curative instinct, that is to say the *defensive and offensive instinct* in man becomes soft. One does not know how to get free of anything, one does not know how to have done with anything, one does not know how to thrust back – everything hurts. Men and things come importunately close, events strike too deep, the memory is a festering wound. Being sick *is* itself a kind of *ressentiment*. – Against this the invalid has only one great means of cure – I call it *Russian fatalism*, that fatalism without rebellion with which a Russian soldier for whom the campaign has become too much at last lies down in the snow. No longer to take anything at all, to receive anything, to take anything *into* oneself – no longer to react at all . . . The great rationality of this fatalism, which is not always the courage to die but can be life-preservative under conditions highly danger- ous to life, is reduction of the metabolism, making it slow down, a kind of will to hibernation. A couple of steps further in this logic and one has the fakir who sleeps for weeks on end in a grave . . . Because one would use oneself up too quickly *if* one reacted at all, one no longer reacts: this is the logic. And nothing burns one up quicker than the affects of *ressentiment*. Vexation, morbid susceptibility, incapacity for revenge, the desire, the thirst for revenge, poison-brewing in any sense – for one who is exhausted this is certainly the most disadvantageous kind of reaction: it causes a rapid expenditure of nervous energy, a morbid accretion of excretions, for example of gall into the stomach. *Ressentiment* is the forbidden *in itself* for the invalid – *his* evil: unfortunately also his most natural inclination. – This was grasped by that profound physiologist Buddha. His 'religion', which one would do better to call a *system of hygiene* so as not to mix it up with such pitiable things as Christianity, makes its effect dependent on victory over *ressentiment*: to free the soul of *that* – first step to recovery. 'Not by enmity is enmity ended, by friendship is enmity ended': this stands at the beginning of Buddha's teaching – it is *not* morality that speaks thus, it is physiology that speaks thus. – *Ressentiment*, born of weakness, to no one more harmful than to the weak man himself – in the opposite case, where a rich nature is the presupposition, a *superfluous* feeling to stay master of which is almost the proof of richness. He who knows the seriousness with which my philosophy has taken up the struggle against the feelings of vengefulness and vindictiveness even into the theory of 'free will' – my struggle against Christianity is only a special instance of it – will understand why it is precisely here that I throw the light on my personal bearing, my *sureness of instinct* in practice. In periods of *décadence* I *forbade* them to myself as harmful; as soon as life was again sufficiently rich and proud for them I forbade them to myself as *beneath* me. That 'Russian fatalism' of which I spoke came forward in my case in the form of clinging tenaciously for years on end to almost intolerable situations, places, residences, company, once chance had placed me in them – it was better than changing them, than *feeling* them as capable of being changed – than rebelling against them ... In those days I took it deadly amiss if I was disturbed in this fatalism, if I was forcibly awakened from it – and to do this was in fact every time a deadly dangerous thing. – To accept oneself as a fate, not to desire oneself 'different' – in such conditions this is *great rationality* itself.

7

War is another thing. I am by nature warlike. To attack is among my instincts. *To be able* to be an enemy, to be an enemy

– that perhaps presupposes a strong nature, it is in any event a condition of every strong nature. It needs resistances, consequently it *seeks* resistances: the *aggressive* pathos belongs as necessarily to strength as the feeling of vengefulness and vindictiveness does to weakness. Woman, for example, is vengeful: that is conditioned by her weakness, just as is her susceptibility to others' distress. – The strength of one who attacks has in the opposition he needs a kind of *gauge*; every growth reveals itself in the seeking out of a powerful opponent – or problem: for a philosopher who is warlike also challenges problems to a duel. The undertaking is to master, *not* any resistances that happen to present themselves, but those against which one has to bring all one's strength, suppleness and mastery of weapons – to master *equal* opponents ... Equality in face of the enemy – first presupposition of an *honest* duel. Where one despises one *cannot* wage war; where one commands, where one sees something as beneath one, one *has* not to wage war. – My practice in warfare can be reduced to four propositions. Firstly: I attack only causes that are victorious – under certain circumstances I wait until they are victorious. Secondly: I attack only causes against which I would find no allies, where I stand alone – where I compromise only myself ... I have never taken a step in public which was not compromising: that is *my* criterion of right action. Thirdly: I never attack persons – I only employ the person as a strong magnifying glass with which one can make visible a general but furtive state of distress which is hard to get hold of. That was how I attacked David Strauss, more precisely the *success* with German 'culture' of a senile book – I thus caught that culture red-handed ... That was how I attacked Wagner, more precisely the falseness, the hybrid instincts of our 'culture' which confuses the artful with the rich, the late with the great. Fourthly: I attack only things where any kind of personal difference is excluded, where there is no background of bad experience. On the contrary, to attack is with me a proof of good will, under certain circumstances of gratitude. I do honour, I confer distinction when I associate my name with a cause, a person: for or against – that is in this regard a matter of indifference to me. If I wage war on Christianity I have a right to do so, because I have never experienced anything disagreeable or frustrating from that direction – the most serious Christians have always been well disposed towards me. I myself, an opponent of Christianity *de rigueur*, am far from bearing a grudge against the individual for what is the fatality of millennia. –

8

May I venture to indicate one last trait of my nature which creates for me no little difficulty in my relations with others? I possess a perfectly uncanny sensitivity of the instinct for cleanliness, so that I perceive physiologically – *smell* – the proximity or – what am I saying? – the innermost parts, the 'entrails', of every soul . . . I have in this sensitivity psychological antennae with which I touch and take hold of every secret: all the *concealed* dirt at the bottom of many a nature, perhaps conditioned by bad blood but whitewashed by education, is known to me almost on first contact. If I have observed correctly, such natures unendurable to my sense of cleanliness for their part also sense the caution of my disgust: they do not thereby become any sweeter-smelling . . . As has always been customary with me – an extreme cleanliness in relation to me is a presupposition of my existence, I perish under unclean conditions – I swim and bathe and splash continually as it were in water, in any kind of perfectly transparent and glittering element. This makes traffic with people no small test of my patience; my humanity consists, *not* in feeling for and with man, but in *enduring* that I do feel for and with him . . . My humanity is a continual self-overcoming. – But I have need of *solitude*, that is to say recovery, return to myself, the breath of a free light playful air . . . My entire Zarathustra is a dithyramb on solitude or, if I have been understood, on *cleanliness* . . . Fortunately not on *pure folly*. – He who has eyes for colours will call it diamond.

– *Disgust* at mankind, at the 'rabble', has always been my greatest danger ... Do you want to hear the words in which Zarathustra speaks of *redemption* from disgust?

Yet what happened to me? How did I free myself from disgust? Who rejuvenated my eyes? How did I fly to the height where the rabble no longer sit at the well?

Did my disgust itself create wings and water-diving powers for me? Truly, I had to fly to the extremest height to find again the fountain of delight!

Oh, I have found it, my brothers! Here, in the extremest height, the fountain of delight gushes up for me! And here there is a life at which no rabble drinks with me!

You gush up almost too impetuously, fountain of delight! And in wanting to fill the cup, you often empty it again.

And I still have to learn to approach you more discreetly: my heart still flows towards you all too impetuously: –

my heart, upon which my summer burns, a short, hot, melancholy, over-joyful summer: how my summer-heart longs for your coolness!

Gone is the lingering affliction of my spring! Gone the snowflakes of my malice in June! Summer have I become entirely, and summer-noonday –

– a summer at the extremest height with cold fountains and blissful stillness: oh come, my friends, that the stillness may become more blissful yet!

For this is *our* height and our home: we live too nobly and boldly here for all unclean men and their thirsts.

Only cast your pure eyes into the well of my delight, friends! You will not dim its sparkle! It shall laugh back at you with *its* purity.

We build our nest in the tree Future: eagles shall bring food to us solitaries in their beaks!

Truly, food in which no unclean men could join us! They would think they were eating fire and burn their mouths.

Truly, we do not prepare a home here for unclean men!

Their bodies and their spirits would call our happiness a cave of ice!

So let us live above them like strong winds, neighbours of the eagles, neighbours of the snow, neighbours of the sun: that is how strong winds live.

And like a wind will I one day blow among them and with my spirit take away the breath of their spirit: thus my future will have it.

Truly, Zarathustra is a strong wind to all flatlands; and he offers this advice to his enemies and to all that spews and spits: take care not to spit *against* the wind! . . .

WHY I AM SO CLEVER

I

— Why do I know a few *more* things? Why am I so clever altogether? I have never reflected on questions that are none — I have not squandered myself. — I have, for example, no experience of actual *religious* difficulties. I am entirely at a loss to know to what extent I ought to have felt 'sinful'. I likewise lack a reliable criterion of a pang of conscience: from what one *hears* of it, a pang of conscience does not seem to me anything respectable ... I should not like to leave an act in the lurch *afterwards*, I would as a matter of principle prefer to leave the evil outcome, the *consequences*, out of the question of values. When the outcome is evil one can easily lose the *true* eye for what one has done: a pang of conscience seems to me a kind of '*evil* eye'. To honour to oneself something that went wrong all the more *because* it went wrong — that rather would accord with my morality. — 'God', 'immortality of the soul', 'redemption', 'the Beyond', all of them concepts to which I have given no attention and no time, not even as a child — perhaps I was never childish enough for it? — I have absolutely no knowledge of atheism as an outcome of reasoning, still less as an event: with me it is obvious by instinct. I am too inquisitive, too *questionable*, too high spirited to rest content with a crude answer. God is a crude answer, a piece of indelicacy against us thinkers — fundamentally even a crude *prohibition* to us: you shall not think! ... I am interested in quite a different way in a question upon which the 'salvation of mankind' depends far more than it does upon any kind of quaint curiosity of the theologians: the question of *nutriment*. One can for convenience' sake formulate it thus: 'how to nourish yourself so as to attain your maximum of strength, of *virtù* in the Renaissance style, of moraline-free virtue?' – My experiences here are as bad as they possibly could be; I am astonished that I heard this question so late, that I learned 'reason' from these experiences so late. Only the perfect worthlessness of our German education – its 'idealism' – can to some extent explain to me why on precisely this point I was backward to the point of holiness. This 'education' which from the first teaches one to lose sight of *realities* so as to hunt after altogether problematic, so-called 'ideal' objectives, 'classical education' for example – as if it were not from the first an utterly fruitless undertaking to try to unite 'classical' and 'German' in *one* concept! It is, moreover, mirth-provoking – just think of a 'classically educated' Leipziger! – Until my very maturest years I did in fact eat *badly* – in the language of morals 'impersonally', 'selflessly', 'altruistically', for the salvation of cooks and other fellow Christians. With the aid of Leipzig cookery, for example, which accompanied my earliest study of Schopenhauer (1865), I very earnestly denied my 'will to live'. To ruin one's stomach so as to receive inadequate nutriment – the aforesaid cookery seems to me to solve this problem wonderfully well. (It is said that 1866 produced a change in this domain –.) But German cookery in general – what does it not have on its conscience! Soup *before* the meal (in Venetian cookery books of the sixteenth century still called *alla tedesca*); meat cooked to shreds, greasy and floury vegetables; the degeneration of puddings to paperweights! If one adds to this the downright bestial dinner-drinking habits of the ancient and by no means only the *ancient* Germans one will also understand the origin of the *German spirit* – disturbed intestines ... The German spirit is an indigestion, it can have done with nothing. – But to the *English* diet too, which compared with the Germans, even with the French, is a kind of 'return to nature', that is to say to cannibalism, my own instinct is profoundly opposed; it seems to me to give the spirit *heavy* feet – the feet of Englishwomen ... The best cookery is that of *Piedmont*. Alcoholic drinks are no good for me; a glass of wine or beer a day is quite enough to make life for me a 'Vale of Tears' – Munich is where my antipodes live. Granted I was a little late to grasp this – I *experienced* it really from childhood onwards. As a boy I believed wine-drinking to be, like tobacco-smoking, at first only a vanity of young men, later a habit. Perhaps the wine of Naumburg is in part to blame for this *austere* judgement. To believe that wine *makes cheerful* I would have to be a Christian, that is to say believe what is for precisely me an absurdity. Oddly enough, while I am put extremely out of sorts by *small*, much diluted doses of alcohol, I am almost turned into a sailor when it comes to *strong* doses. Even as a boy I showed how brave I was in this respect. To write a long Latin essay in a *single* night's sitting and then go on to make a fair copy of it, with the ambition in my pen to imitate in severity and concision my model Sallust, and to pour a quantity of grog of the heaviest calibre over my Latin, was even when I was a pupil of venerable Schulpforta in no way opposed to my physiology, nor perhaps to that of Sallust – however much it might have been to venerable Schulpforta ... Later, towards the middle of life, I decided, to be sure, more and more strictly *against* any sort of 'spirituous' drink: an opponent of vegetarianism from experience, just like Richard Wagner, who converted me, I cannot advise all *more spiritual* natures too seriously to abstain from alcohol absolutely. *Water* suffices ... I prefer places in which there is everywhere opportunity to drink from flowing fountains (Nice, Turin, Sils); a small glass runs after me like a dog. *In vino veritas*: it seems that here too I am again at odds with all the world over the concept 'truth' – with me the spirit moves over the water ... A couple more signposts from my morality. A big meal is easier to digest than one too small. That the stomach comes into action as a whole, first precondition of a good digestion. One has to *know* the size of one's stomach. For the same reason those tedious meals should be avoided which I call interrupted sacrificial feasts, those at the *table d'hôte*. – No eating between meals, no coffee: coffee makes gloomy.

Tea beneficial only in the morning. Little, but strong: tea very detrimental and sicklying o'er the whole day if it is the slightest bit too weak. Each has here his own degree, often between the narrowest and most delicate limits. In a very *agaçant* climate it is inadvisable to start with tea: one should start an hour earlier with a cup of thick oil-free cocoa. – *Sit* as little as possible; credit no thought not born in the open air and while moving freely about – in which the muscles too do not hold a festival. All prejudices come from the intestines. – Assiduity – I have said it once before – the actual *sin* against the holy spirit. –

2

Most closely related to the question of nutriment is the question of *place* and *climate*. No one is free to live everywhere; and he who has great tasks to fulfil which challenge his entire strength has indeed in this matter a very narrow range of choice. The influence of climate on the *metabolism*, its slowing down, its speeding up, extends so far that a blunder in regard to place and climate can not only estrange anyone from his task but withhold it from him altogether: he never catches sight of it. His animalic *vigor* never grows sufficiently great for him to attain to that freedom overflowing into the most spiritual domain where he knows: *that* I alone can do ... A never so infinitesimal sluggishness of the intestines grown into a bad habit completely suffices to transform a genius into something mediocre, something 'German'; the German climate alone is enough to discourage strong and even heroic intestines. The *tempo* of the metabolism stands in an exact relationship to the mobility or lameness of the *feet* of the spirit; the 'spirit' itself is indeed only a species of this metabolism. Make a list of the places where there are and have been gifted men, where wit, refinement, malice are a part of happiness, where genius has almost necessarily made its home: they all possess an excellent dry air. Paris, Provence, Florence, Jerusalem, Athens – these names prove something: that genius is *conditioned* by dry air, clear sky – that is to say by rapid metabolism, by the possibility of again and again supplying oneself with great, even tremendous quantities of energy. I have in mind a case in which a spirit which might have become significant and free became instead narrow, withdrawn, a grumpy specialist, merely through a lack of instinctive subtlety in choice of climate. And I myself could in the end have become this case if sickness had not compelled me to reason, to reflect on reason in reality. Now, when from long practice I read climatic and meteorological effects off from myself as from a very delicate and reliable instrument and even on a short journey, from Turin to Milan for instance, verify on myself physiologically the change in degrees of humidity, I recall with horror the *uncanny* fact that my life up to the last ten years, the years when my life was in danger, was spent nowhere but in wrong places downright *forbidden* to me. Naumburg, Schulpforta, Thuringia in general, Leipzig, Basel, Venice – so many ill-fated places for my physiology. If I have no welcome memories at all of my whole childhood and youth, it would be folly to attribute this to so-called 'moral' causes – the undeniable lack of *adequate* company, for instance: for this lack exists today as it has always existed without preventing me from being brave and cheerful. Ignorance *in physiologis* – accursed 'idealism' – is the real fatality in my life, the superfluous and stupid in it, something out of which nothing good grows, for which there is no compensation, no counter-reckoning. It is as a consequence of this 'idealism' that I elucidate to myself all the blunders, all the great deviations of instinct and 'modesties' which led me away from the *task* of my life, that I became a philologist for example – why not at least a physician or something else that opens the eyes? In my time at Basel my entire spiritual diet, the division of the day included, was a perfectly senseless abuse of extraordinary powers without any kind of provision for covering this consumption, without even reflection on consumption and replacement. Any more subtle selfishness, any *protection* by a commanding instinct was lacking, it was an equating of oneself with everyone else, a piece of 'selflessness', a forgetting of one's distance – something I shall never forgive myself. When I was almost done for, *because* I was almost done for, I began to reflect on this fundamental irrationality of my life – 'idealism'. It was only *sickness* that brought me to reason. –

3

Selectivity in nutriment; selectivity in climate and place; – the third thing in which one may at no cost commit a blunder is selectivity in *one's kind of recreation*. Here too the degree to which a spirit is *sui generis* makes ever narrower the bounds of what is permitted, that is to say *useful* to him. In my case all reading is among my recreations: consequently among those things which free me from myself, which allow me to saunter among strange sciences and souls – which I no longer take seriously. It is precisely reading which helps me to recover from *my* seriousness. At times when I am deeply sunk in work you will see no books around me: I would guard against letting anyone speak or even think in my vicinity. And that is what reading would mean ... Has it really been noticed that in that state of profound tension to which pregnancy condemns the spirit and fundamentally the entire organism, any chance event, any kind of stimulus from without has too vehement an effect, 'cuts' too deeply? One has to avoid the chance event, the stimulus from without, as much as possible; a kind of self-walling-up is among the instinctual sagacities of spiritual pregnancy. Shall I allow a *strange* thought to climb secretly over the wall? – And that is what reading would mean ... The times of work and fruitfulness are followed by the time of recreation: come hither, you pleasant, you witty, you clever books! Will they be German books? ... I have to reckon back half a year to catch myself with a book in my hand. But what was it? – An excellent study by Victor Brochard, *les sceptiques Grecs*, in which my Laertiana are also well employed. The Sceptics, the only *honourable* type among the two- and five-fold ambiguous philosophical crowd! ... Otherwise I take flight almost always to the same books, really a small number, those books which have *proved* themselves precisely to me. It does not perhaps lie in my nature to read much or many kinds of things: a reading room makes me ill. Neither does it lie in my nature to love much or many kinds of things. Caution, even hostility towards new books is rather part of my instinct than 'tolerance', '*largeur du coeur*' and other forms of 'neighbour love' ... It is really only a small number of older Frenchmen to whom I return again and again: I believe only in French culture and consider everything in Europe that calls itself 'culture' a misunderstanding, not to speak of German culture ... The few instances of high culture I have encountered in Germany have all been of French origin, above all Frau Cosima Wagner, by far the first voice I have heard in questions of taste. – That I do not read Pascal but *love* him, as the most instructive of all sacrifices to Christianity, slowly murdered first physically then psychologically, the whole logic of this most horrible form of inhuman cruelty; that I have something of Montaigne's wantonness in my spirit, who knows? perhaps also in my body; that my artist's taste defends the names Molière, Corneille and Racine, not without wrath, against a disorderly genius such as Shakespeare: this does not ultimately exclude my finding the most recent Frenchmen also charming company. I cannot at all conceive in which century of history one could haul together such inquisitive and at the same time such delicate psychologists as one can in contemporary Paris: I name as a sample – for their number is by no means small, Messrs Paul Bourget, Pierre Loti, Gyp, Meilhac, Anatole France, Jules Lemaitre, or to pick out one of the stronger race, a genuine Latin to whom I am especially attached, Guy de Maupassant. Between ourselves, I prefer *this* generation even to their great teachers, who have all been ruined by German philosophy (M. Taine for example by Hegel, whom he has to thank for this misunderstanding of great human beings and ages). As far as Germany extends it *ruins* culture. It was only the war that 'redeemed' the spirit in France ... Stendhal, one of the fairest accidents of my life – for whatever marks an epoch in my life has been brought to me by accident, never by a recommendation – is utterly invaluable with his anticipating psychologist's eye, with his grasp of facts which reminds one of the proximity of the greatest man of the factual (*ex ungue Napoleonem* –); finally not least as an *honest* atheist, a rare, almost undiscoverable species in France – with all deference to *Prosper Mérimée* . . . Perhaps I am even envious of Stendhal? He robbed me of the best atheist joke which precisely I could have made: 'God's only excuse is that he does not exist' . . . I myself have said somewhere: what has hitherto been the greatest objection to existence? *God* . . .

4

The highest conception of the lyric poet was given me by *Heinrich Heine*. I seek in vain in all the realms of millennia for an equally sweet and passionate music. He possesses that divine malice without which I cannot imagine perfection – I assess the value of people, of races according to how necessarily they are unable to separate the god from the satyr. – And how he employs German! It will one day be said that Heine and I have been by far the first artists of the German language – at an incalculable distance from everything which mere Germans have done with it. – I must be profoundly related to *Byron's* Manfred: I discovered all these abysses in myself – I was ripe for this work at thirteen. I have no words, only a look for those who dare to say the word Faust in the presence of Manfred. The Germans are *incapable* of any conception of greatness: proof Schumann. Expressly from wrath against this sugary Saxon, I composed a counter-overture to Manfred, of which Hans von Bülow said he had never seen the like on manuscript paper: it constituted a rape on Euterpe. – When I seek my highest formula for *Shakespeare* I find it always in that he conceived the type of Caesar. One cannot guess at things like this – one is it or one is not. The great poet creates *only* out of his own reality – to the point at which he is afterwards unable to endure his own work ... When I have taken a glance at my Zarathustra I walk up and down my room for half an hour unable to master an unendurable spasm of sobbing. – I know of no more heartrending reading than Shakespeare: what must a man have suffered to need to be a buffoon to this extent! – Is Hamlet *understood*? It is not doubt, it is *certainty* which makes mad ... But to feel in this way one must be profound, abyss, philosopher ... We all *fear* truth ... And, to confess it: I am instinctively certain that Lord Bacon is the originator, the self-tormentor of this uncanniest species of literature: what do *I* care about the pitiable chatter of American shallow-pates and muddle-heads? But the power for the mightiest reality of vision is not only compatible with the mightiest power for action, for the monstrous in action, for crime – *it even presupposes it* ... We do not know nearly enough about Lord Bacon, the first realist in every great sense of the word, to know *what* he did, *what* he wanted, *what* he experienced within himself ... And the devil take it, my dear critics! Supposing I had baptized my Zarathustra with another name, for example with the name of Richard Wagner, the perspicuity of two millennia would not have sufficed to divine that the author of 'Human, All Too Human' is the visionary of Zarathustra ...

5

Here where I am speaking of the recreations of my life, I need to say a word to express my gratitude for that which of all things in it has refreshed me by far the most profoundly and cordially. This was without any doubt my intimate association with Richard Wagner. I offer all my other human relationships cheap; but at no price would I relinquish from my life the Tribschen days, those days of mutual confidences, of cheerfulness, of sublime incidents – of *profound* moments ... I do not know what others may have experienced with Wagner: over *our* sky no cloud ever passed. – And with that I return again to

France – I cannot spare reasons, I can spare a mere curl of the lip for Wagnerians *et hoc genus omne* who believe they are doing honour to Wagner when they find him similar to *themselves* . . . Constituted as I am, a stranger in my deepest instincts to everything German, so that the mere presence of a German hinders my digestion, my first contact with Wagner was also the first time in my life I ever drew a deep breath: I felt, I reverenced him as a being from *outside*, as the opposite, the incarnate protest against all 'German virtues'. – We who were children in the swamp-air of the fifties are necessarily pessimists regarding the concept 'German'; we cannot be anything but revolutionaries – we shall acquiesce in no state of things in which the *bigot* is on top. It is a matter of complete indifference to me if today he plays in different colours, if he dresses in scarlet and dons the uniform of a hussar . . . Very well! Wagner was a revolutionary – he fled from the Germans . . . As an *artist* one has no home in Europe except in Paris: the *delicatesse* in all five senses of art which Wagner's art presupposes, the fingers for nuances, the psychological morbidity, is to be found only in Paris. Nowhere else does there exist such a passion in questions of form, this seriousness in *mise en scène* – it is the Parisian seriousness *par excellence*. There is in Germany absolutely no conception of the tremendous ambition which dwells in the soul of a Parisian artist. The German is good-natured – Wagner was by no means good-natured . . . But I have already said sufficient (in 'Beyond Good and Evil' §256) as to where Wagner belongs, in whom he has his closest relatives: the French late romantics, that high-flying and yet exhilarating kind of artists such as Delacroix, such as Berlioz, with a *fond* of sickness, of incurability in their nature, sheer fanatics for *expression*, virtuosi through and through . . . Who was the first *intelligent* adherent of Wagner? Charles Baudelaire, the same as was the first to understand Delacroix, that typical *décadent* in whom an entire race of artists recognized themselves – he was perhaps also the last . . . What I have never forgiven Wagner? That he *condescended* to the Germans – that he became *reichsdeutsch* . . . As far as Germany extends it *ruins* culture. –

6

All in all I could not have endured my youth without Wagnerian music. For I was *condemned* to Germans. If one wants to get free from an unendurable pressure one needs hashish. Very well, I needed Wagner. Wagner is the counter-poison to everything German *par excellence* – still poison, I do not dispute it ... From the moment there was a piano score of Tristan – my compliments, Herr von Bülow! – I was a Wagnerian. The earliest works of Wagner I saw as beneath me – still too common, too 'German' ... But I still today seek a work of a dangerous fascination, of a sweet and shuddery infinity equal to that of Tristan – I seek in all the arts in vain. All the strangenesses of Leonardo da Vinci lose their magic at the first note of Tristan. This work is altogether Wagner's *non plus ultra*; he recuperated from it with the Meistersinger and the Ring. To become healthier – that is *retrogression* in the case of a nature such as Wagner ... I take it for a piece of good fortune of the first rank to have lived at the right time, and to have lived precisely among Germans, so as to be *ripe* for this work: my psychologist's inquisitiveness goes that far. The world is poor for him who has never been sick enough for this 'voluptuousness of hell': to employ a mystic's formula is permissible, almost obligatory, here. I think I know better than anyone what tremendous things Wagner was capable of, the fifty worlds of strange delights to which no one but he had wings; and as I am strong enough to turn even the most questionable and most perilous things to my own advantage and thus to become stronger, I call Wagner the great benefactor of my life. That in which we are related, that we have suffered more profoundly, from one another also, than men of this century are capable of suffering, will eternally join our names together again and again; and as surely as Wagner is among Germans merely a misunderstanding, just as surely am I and always will be. – Two centuries of psychological and artistic discipline *first*, my Herr Germans! ... But one cannot catch up that amount. –

7

– I shall say another word for the most select ears: what I really want from music. That it is cheerful and profound, like an afternoon in October. That it is individual, wanton, tender, a little sweet woman of lowness and charm ... I shall never admit that a German *could* know what music is. What one calls German musicians, the greatest above all, are *foreigners*, Slavs, Croats, Italians, Netherlanders – or Jews: otherwise Germans of the strong race, *extinct* Germans, like Heinrich Schütz, Bach and Handel. I myself am still sufficient of a Pole to exchange the rest of music for Chopin; for three reasons I exclude Wagner's Siegfried Idyll, perhaps also a few things by Liszt, who excels all other musicians in the nobility of his orchestral tone; finally all that has grown up beyond the Alps – *this side* ... I would not know how to get on without Rossini, even less without *my* south in music, the music of my Venetian *maestro Pietro Gasti*. And when I say beyond the Alps I am really saying only Venice. When I seek another word for music I never find any other word than Venice. I do not know how to distinguish between tears and music – I do not know how to think of happiness, of the *south*, without a shudder of faintheartedness.

> Lately I stood at the bridge
> in the brown night.
> From afar there came a song:
> a golden drop, it swelled
> across the trembling surface.
> Gondolas, lights, music –
> drunken it swam out into the gloom ...
> My soul, a stringed instrument,
> touched by invisible hands
> sang to itself in reply a gondola song,
> and trembled with gaudy happiness.
> – Was anyone listening?

8

In all this – in selection of nutriment, of place and climate, of recreation – there commands an instinct of self-preservation which manifests itself most unambiguously as an instinct for *self-defence*. Not to see many things, not to hear them, not to let them approach one – first piece of ingenuity, first proof that one is no accident but a necessity. The customary word for this self-defensive instinct is *taste*. Its imperative commands, not only to say No when Yes would be a piece of 'selflessness', but also to say *No as little as possible*. To separate oneself, to depart from that to which No would be required again and again. The rationale is that defensive expenditures, be they never so small, become a rule, a habit, lead to an extraordinary and perfectly superfluous impoverishment. Our *largest* expenditures are our most frequent small ones. Warding off, not letting come close, is an expenditure – one should not deceive oneself over this – a strength *squandered* on negative objectives. One can merely through the constant need to ward off become too weak any longer to defend oneself. – Suppose I were to step out of my house and discover, instead of calm and aristocratic Turin, the German provincial town: my instinct would have to blockade itself so as to push back all that pressed upon it from this flat and cowardly world. Or suppose I discovered the German metropolis, that builded vice where nothing grows, where every kind of thing, good and bad, is dragged in. Would I not in face of it have to become a *hedgehog*? – But to have spikes is an extravagance, a double luxury even if one is free to have no spikes but *open* hands . . .

Another form of sagacity and self-defence consists in *reacting as seldom as possible* and withdrawing from situations and relationships in which one would be condemned as it were to suspend one's 'freedom', one's initiative, and become a mere reagent. I take as a parable traffic with books. The scholar, who really does nothing but 'trundle' books – the philologist at a modest assessment about 200 a day – finally loses altogether the ability to think for himself. If he does not trundle he does not think. He *replies* to a stimulus (– a thought he has read) when he thinks – finally he does nothing but react. The scholar expends his entire strength in affirmation and denial, in criticizing what has already been thought – he himself no longer thinks . . . The instinct for self-defence has in his case become soft; otherwise he would defend himself against books. The scholar – a *décadent*. – This I have seen with my own eyes: natures gifted, rich and free already in their thirties 'read to ruins', mere matches that have to be struck if they are to ignite – emit 'thoughts'. – Early in the morning at the break of day, in all the freshness and dawn of one's strength, to read a *book* – I call that vicious! –

9

At this point I can no longer avoid actually answering the question *how one becomes what one is*. And with that I touch on the masterpiece in the art of self-preservation – of *selfishness* . . . For assuming that the task, the vocation, the *destiny* of the task exceeds the average measure by a significant degree, there would be no greater danger than to catch sight of oneself *with* this task. That one becomes what one is presupposes that one does not have the remotest idea *what* one is. From this point of view even the *blunders* of life – the temporary sidepaths and wrong turnings, the delays, the 'modesties', the seriousness squandered on tasks which lie outside *the* task – have their own meaning and value. They are an expression of a great sagacity, even the supreme sagacity: where *nosce te ipsum* would be the recipe for destruction, self-forgetfulness, self-*misunderstanding*, self-diminution, -narrowing, -mediocratizing becomes reason itself. Expressed morally: love of one's neighbour, living for others and other things *can* be the defensive measure for the preservation of the sternest selfishness. This is the exceptional case in which I, contrary to my rule and conviction, take the side of the 'selfless' drives: here they work in the service of *selfishness, self-cultivation*. – The entire surface of consciousness –

consciousness *is* a surface – has to be kept clear of any of the
great imperatives. Even the grand words, the grand attitudes
must be guarded against! All of them represent a danger that
the instinct will 'understand itself' too early – –. In the meantime
the organizing 'idea' destined to rule grows and grows in the
depths – it begins to command, it slowly leads *back* from
sidepaths and wrong turnings, it prepares *individual* qualities
and abilities which will one day prove themselves indispensable
as means to achieving the whole – it constructs the *ancillary*
capacities one after the other before it gives any hint of the
dominating task, of the 'goal', 'objective', 'meaning'. – Regarded from this side my life is simply wonderful. For the task
of a *revaluation of values* more capacities perhaps were required
than have dwelt together in one individual, above all antithetical
capacities which however are not allowed to disturb or destroy
one another. Order of rank among capacities; distance; the art
of dividing without making inimical; mixing up nothing, 'recon-
ciling' nothing; a tremendous multiplicity which is none the less
the opposite of chaos – this has been the precondition, the
protracted secret labour and artistic working of my instinct.
The magnitude of its *higher protection* was shown in the fact I
have at no time had the remotest idea what was growing within
me – that all my abilities one day *leapt forth* suddenly ripe, in
their final perfection. I cannot remember ever having taken any
trouble – no trace of *struggle* can be discovered in my life, I am
the opposite of an heroic nature. To 'want' something, to
'strive' after something, to have a 'goal', a 'wish' in view – I
know none of this from experience. Even at this moment I
look out upon my future – a *distant* future! – as upon a smooth
sea: it is ruffled by no desire. I do not want in the slightest that
anything should become other than it is; I do not want myself
to become other than I am . . . But that is how I have always
lived. I have harboured no desire. Someone who after his forty-
fourth year can say he has never striven after *honours*, after
women, after *money*! – Not that I could not have had them . . .
Thus, for example, I one day became a university professor – I

had never had the remotest thought of such a thing, for I was barely twenty-four years old. Thus two years earlier I was one day a philologist: in the sense that my *first* philological work, my beginning in any sense, was requested by my teacher Ritschl for his 'Rheinisches Museum' (*Ritschl* – I say it with respect – the only scholar gifted with genius whom I have encountered up to the present day. He was characterized by that pleasant depravity which distinguishes us Thuringians and which can render even a German sympathetic – to get to the truth we even prefer to go by secret paths. I should not with these words like to have in any way undervalued my close compatriot, the *sagacious* Leopold von Ranke . . .)

10

– I shall be asked why I have really narrated all these little things which according to the traditional judgement are matters of indifference: it will be said that in doing so I harm myself all the more if I am destined to fulfil great tasks. Answer: these little things – nutriment, place, climate, recreation, the whole casuistry of selfishness – are beyond all conception of greater importance than anything that has been considered of importance hitherto. It is precisely here that one has to begin to *learn anew*. Those things which mankind has hitherto pondered seriously are not even realities, merely imaginings, more strictly speaking *lies* from the bad instincts of sick, in the profoundest sense injurious natures – all the concepts 'God', 'soul', 'virtue', 'sin', 'the Beyond', 'truth', 'eternal life' . . . But the greatness of human nature, its 'divinity', has been sought in them . . . All questions of politics, the ordering of society, education have been falsified down to their foundations because the most injurious men have been taken for great men – because contempt has been taught for the 'little' things, which is to say for the fundamental affairs of life . . . Now, when I compare myself with the men who have hitherto been honoured as *pre-eminent* men the distinction is palpable. I do not count these supposed 'pre-eminent men' as belonging to mankind at all – to me they are the refuse of mankind, abortive offspring of sickness and vengeful instincts: they are nothing but pernicious, fundamentally incurable monsters who take revenge on life . . . I want to be the antithesis of this: it is my privilege to possess the highest subtlety for all the signs of healthy instincts. Every morbid trait is lacking in me; even in periods of severe illness I did not become morbid; a trait of fanaticism will be sought in vain in my nature. At no moment of my life can I be shown to have adopted any kind of arrogant or pathetic posture. The pathos of attitudes does *not* belong to greatness; whoever needs attitudes at all is *false* . . . Beware of all picturesque men! – Life has been easy for me, easiest when it demanded of me the most difficult things. Anyone who saw me during the seventy days of this autumn when I was uninterruptedly creating nothing but things of the first rank which no man will be able to do again or has done before, bearing a responsibility for all the coming millennia, will have noticed no trace of tension in me, but rather an overflowing freshness and cheerfulness. I never ate with greater relish, I never slept better. – I know of no other way of dealing with great tasks than that of *play*: this is, as a sign of greatness, an essential precondition. The slightest constraint, the gloomy mien, any kind of harsh note in the throat are all objections to a man, how much more to his work! . . . One must have no nerves . . . To *suffer* from solitude is likewise an objection – I have always suffered only from the 'multitude' . . . At an absurdly early age, at the age of seven, I already knew that no human word would ever reach me: has anyone ever seen me sad on that account? – Still today I treat everyone with the same geniality, I am even full of consideration for the basest people: in all this there is not a grain of arrogance, of secret contempt. He whom I despise *divines* that I despise him: through my mere existence I enrage everything that has bad blood in its veins . . . My formula for greatness in a human being is *amor fati*: that one wants nothing to be other than it is, not in the future, not in the past, not in all eternity. Not merely

to endure that which happens of necessity, still less to dissemble
it — all idealism is untruthfulness in the face of necessity — but
to *love* it . . .

WHY I WRITE SUCH
GOOD BOOKS

I

I AM one thing, my writings are another. – Here, before I speak of these writings themselves, I shall touch on the question of their being understood or *not* understood. I shall do so as perfunctorily as is fitting: for the time for this question has certainly not yet come. My time has not yet come, some are born posthumously. – One day or other institutions will be needed in which people live and teach as I understand living and teaching: perhaps even chairs for the interpretation of Zarathustra will be established. But it would be a complete contradiction of myself if I expected ears *and hands* for *my* truths already today: that I am not heard today, that no one today knows how to take from me, is not only comprehensible; it even seems to me right. I do not want to be taken for what I am not – and that requires that I do not take myself for what I am not. To say it again, little of 'ill will' can be shown in my life; neither would I be able to speak of barely a single case of 'literary ill will'. On the other hand all too much of *pure folly*! ... It seems to me that to take a book of mine into his hands is one of the rarest distinctions anyone can confer upon himself – I even assume he removes his shoes when he does so – not to speak of boots ... When Doctor Heinrich von Stein once honestly complained that he understood not one word of my Zarathustra, I told him that was quite in order: to have understood, that is to say *experienced*, six sentences of that book would raise one to a higher level of mortals than 'modern' man could attain to. How *could* I, with *this* feeling of distance, even want the 'modern men' I know – to read me! – My triumph is precisely the opposite of Schopenhauer's – I say 'non *legor*, non *legar*'. – Not that I should like to underestimate the pleasure which the *innocence* in the rejection of my writings has given me. This very summer just gone, at a time when, with my own weighty, too heavily weighty literature, I was perhaps throwing all the rest of literature off its balance, a professor of Berlin University kindly gave me to understand that I ought really to avail myself of a different form: no one read stuff like mine. – In the end it was not Germany but Switzerland which offered me the two extreme cases. An essay of Dr V. Widmann in the *Bund* on 'Beyond Good and Evil' under the title 'Nietzsche's Dangerous Book', and a general report on my books as a whole on the part of Herr Karl Spitteler, also in the *Bund*, constitute a maximum in my life – of what I take care not to say ... The latter, for example, dealt with my Zarathustra as an *advanced exercise in style*, with the request that I might later try to provide some content; Dr Widmann expressed his respect for the courage with which I strive to abolish all decent feelings. – Through a little trick of chance every sentence here was, with a consistency I had to admire, a truth stood on its head: remarkably enough, all one had to do was to 'revalue all values' in order to hit the nail on the head with regard to me – instead of hitting my head with a nail ... All the more reason for me to attempt an explanation. – Ultimately, no one can extract from things, books included, more than he already knows. What one has no access to through experience one has no ear for. Now let us imagine an extreme case: that a book speaks of nothing but events which lie outside the possibility of general or even of rare experience – that it is the *first* language for a new range of experiences. In this case simply nothing will be heard, with the acoustical illusion that where nothing is heard there *is* nothing ... This is in fact my average experience and, if you like, the *originality* of my experience. Whoever believed he had understood something of me had dressed up something out of me after his own image – not uncommonly an antithesis of me, for instance an 'idealist'; whoever had understood nothing of me denied that I came into consideration at all. – The word 'superman' to designate a type that has turned out supremely well, in antithesis to 'modern' men, to 'good' men, to Christians and other nihilists – a word which, in the mouth of a Zarathustra, the *destroyer* of morality, becomes a very thoughtful word – has almost everywhere been understood with perfect innocence in the sense of those values whose antithesis makes its appearance in the figure of Zarathustra: that is to say as an 'idealistic' type of higher species of man, half 'saint', half 'genius' ... Other learned cattle caused me on its account to be suspected of Darwinism; even the 'hero cult' of that great unconscious and involuntary counterfeiter Carlyle which I rejected so maliciously has been recognized in it. He into whose ear I whispered he ought to look around rather for a Cesare Borgia than for a Parsifal did not believe his ears. – That I am utterly incurious about discussions of my books, especially by newspapers, will have to be forgiven me. My friends, my publishers know this and do not speak to me about such things. In a particular instance I once had a sight of all the sins that had been committed against a single book – it was 'Beyond Good and Evil'; I could tell a pretty story about that. Would you believe it that the 'Nationalzeitung' – a Prussian newspaper, for my foreign readers – I myself read, if I may say so, only the Journal des Débats – could in all seriousness understand the book as a 'sign of the times', as the real genuine *Junker philosophy* for which the 'Kreuzzeitung' merely lacked the courage? ...

2

This was said for Germans: for I have readers everywhere else – nothing but *choice* intelligences of proved character brought up in high positions and duties; I have even real geniuses among my readers. In Vienna, in St Petersburg, in Stockholm, in Copenhagen, in Paris and New York – I have been discovered everywhere: I have *not* been in Europe's flatland Germany ...

And to confess it, I rejoice even more over my non-readers, such as have never heard either my name or the word philosophy; but wherever I go, here in Turin for example, every face grows more cheerful and benevolent at the sight of me. What has flattered me the most is that old market-women take great pains to select together for me the sweetest of their grapes. That is *how far* one must be a philosopher ... It is not in vain that the Poles are called the French among the Slavs. A charming Russian lady would not mistake for a moment where I belong. I cannot succeed in becoming solemn, the most I can achieve is embarrassment ... To think German, to feel German – I can do everything, but *that* is beyond my powers ... My old teacher Ritschl went so far as to maintain that I conceived even my philological essays like a Parisian *romancier* – absurdly exciting. In Paris itself there is astonishment over *'toutes mes audaces et finesses'* – the expression is Monsieur Taine's –; I fear that with me there is up to the highest forms of the dithyramb an admixture of that salt which never gets soggy – 'German' – *esprit* ... I cannot do otherwise, so help me God! Amen. – We all know, some even know from experience, what a longears is. Very well, I dare to assert that I possess the smallest ears. This is of no little interest to women – it seems to me they feel themselves better understood by me? ... I am the *anti-ass par excellence* and therewith a world-historical monster – I am, in Greek and not only in Greek, the *Anti-Christ* ...

3

I know my privileges as a writer to some extent; in individual cases it has been put to me how greatly habituation to my writings 'ruins' taste. One can simply no longer endure other books, philosophical ones least of all. To enter this noble and delicate world is an incomparable distinction – to do so one absolutely must not be a German; it is in the end a distinction one has to have earned. But he who is related to me through *loftiness* of will experiences when he reads me real ecstasies of

42

learning: for I come from heights no bird has ever soared to, I know abysses into which no foot has ever yet strayed. I have been told it is impossible to put a book of mine down – I even disturb the night's rest . . . There is altogether no prouder and at the same time more exquisite kind of book than my books – they attain here and there the highest thing that can be attained on earth, cynicism; one needs the most delicate fingers as well as the bravest fists if one is to master them. Any infirmity of soul excludes one from them once and for all, any dyspepsia, even, does so: one must have no nerves, one must have a joyful belly. Not only does the poverty, the hole-and-corner air of a soul exclude it from them – cowardice, uncleanliness, secret revengeful- ness in the entrails does so far more: a word from me drives all bad instincts into the face. I have among my acquaintances several experimental animals on whom I bring home to myself the various, very instructively various reactions to my writings. Those who want to have nothing to do with their contents, my so-called friends for example, become 'impersonal': they congratu- late me on having 'done it' again – progress is apparent, too, in a greater cheerfulness of tone . . . The completely vicious 'spirits', the 'beautiful souls', the thoroughly and utterly mendacious have no idea at all what to do with these books – consequently they see the same as *beneath* them, the beautiful consistency of all 'beautiful souls'. The horned cattle among my acquaintances, mere Ger- mans if I may say so, give me to understand they are not always of my opinion, though they are sometimes . . . I have heard this said even of Zarathustra . . . Any 'feminism' in a person, or in a man, likewise closes the gates on me: one will never be able to enter this labyrinth of daring knowledge. One must never have spared oneself, *harshness* must be among one's habits, if one is to be happy and cheerful among nothing but hard truths. When I picture a perfect reader, I always picture a monster of courage and curiosity, also something supple, cunning, cautious, a born adventurer and discoverer. Finally: I would not know how to say better to whom at bottom alone I speak than Zarathustra has said it: *to whom* alone does he want to narrate his riddle?

To you, the bold venturers and adventurers, and whoever has embarked with cunning sails upon dreadful seas,

to you who are intoxicated with riddles, who take pleasure in twilight, whose soul is lured with flutes to every treacherous abyss –

for you do not desire to feel for a rope with cowardly hand; and where you can *guess* you hate to *calculate* . . .

4

I shall at the same time also say a general word on my *art of style*. To *communicate* a state, an inner tension of pathos through signs, including the tempo of these signs – that is the meaning of every style; and considering that the multiplicity of inner states is in my case extraordinary, there exists in my case the possibility of many styles – altogether the most manifold art of style any man ever had at his disposal. Every style is *good* which actually communicates an inner state, which makes no mistake as to the signs, the tempo of the signs, the *gestures* – all rules of phrasing are art of gesture. My instinct is here infallible. – Good style *in itself* – a piece of pure folly, mere 'idealism', on a par with the 'beautiful *in itself*', the 'good *in itself*', the 'thing *in itself*' . . . Always presupposing there are ears – that there are those capable and worthy of a similar pathos, that those are not lacking to whom one *ought* to communicate oneself. – My Zarathustra for example is at present still looking for them – alas! he will have to look for a long time yet! One has to be *worthy* of assaying him . . . And until then there will be no one who comprehends the *art* which has here been squandered: no one has ever had more of the new, the unheard-of, the really new-created in artistic means to squander. That such a thing was possible in the German language remained to be proved: I myself would previously have most hotly disputed it. Before me one did not know what can be done with the German language – what can be done with language as such. The art of *grand* rhythm, the *grand style* of phrasing, as the expression of a

44

tremendous rise and fall of sublime, of superhuman passion, was first discovered by me; with a dithyramb such as the last of the *third* Zarathustra, entitled 'The Seven Seals', I flew a thousand miles beyond that which has hitherto been called poesy.

5

– That out of my writings there speaks a *psychologist* who has not his equal, that is perhaps the first thing a good reader will notice – a reader such as I deserve, who reads me as good old philologists read their Horace. The propositions over which everybody is in fundamental agreement – not to speak of everybody's philosophers, the moralists and other hollow-heads and cabbage-heads – appear with me as naive blunders: for example that belief that 'unegoistic' and 'egoistic' are antitheses, while the *ego* itself is merely a 'higher swindle', an 'ideal'. There are *neither* egoistic *nor* unegoistic actions: both concepts are psychologically nonsense. Or the proposition 'man strives after happiness' ... Or the proposition 'happiness is the reward of virtue' ... Or the proposition 'pleasure and displeasure are opposites' ... The Circe of mankind, morality, has falsified all *psychologica* to its very foundations – has *moralized* it – to the point of the frightful absurdity that love is supposed to be something 'unegoistic' ... One has to be set firmly upon *oneself*, one has to stand bravely upon one's own two legs, otherwise one *cannot* love at all. In the long run the little women know that all too well: they play the deuce with selfless, with merely objective men ... Dare I venture in addition to suggest that I *know* these little women? It is part of my Dionysian endowment. Who knows? perhaps I am the first psychologist of the eternal-womanly. They all love me – an old story: excepting the *abortive* women, the 'emancipated' who lack the stuff for children. – Happily I am not prepared to be torn to pieces: the complete woman tears to pieces when she loves ... I know these amiable maenads ... Ah, what a dangerous, creeping, subterranean little beast of prey it is! And so pleasant with it! ... A little woman chasing after her revenge would over-run fate itself. – The woman is unspeakably more wicked than the man, also cleverer; goodness in a woman is already a form of *degeneration* ... At the bottom of all so-called 'beautiful souls' there lies a physiological disadvantage – I shall not say all I could or I should become medicynical. The struggle for *equal* rights is even a symptom of sickness: every physician knows that. – The more a woman is a woman the more she defends herself tooth and nail against rights in general: for the state of nature, the eternal *war* between the sexes puts her in a superior position by far. – Have there been ears for my definition of love? it is the only one worthy of a philosopher. Love – in its methods war, in its foundation the mortal hatred of the sexes. Has my answer been heard to the question how one cures – 'redeems' – a woman? One makes a child for her. The woman has need of children, the man is always only the means: thus spoke Zarathustra. – 'Emancipation of woman' – is the instinctive hatred of the woman who has *turned out ill*, that is to say is incapable of bearing, for her who has turned out well – the struggle against 'man' is always only means, subterfuge, tactic. When they elevate *themselves* as 'woman in herself', as 'higher woman', as 'idealist' woman, they want to *lower* the general level of rank of woman; no surer means for achieving that than grammar school education, trousers and the political rights of voting cattle. At bottom the emancipated are the *anarchists* in the world of the 'eternal-womanly', the under-privileged whose deepest instinct is revenge ... An entire species of the most malevolent 'idealism' – which, by the way, also occurs in men, for example in the case of Henrik Ibsen, that typical old maid – has the objective of *poisoning* the good conscience, the naturalness in sexual love ... And so as to leave no doubt as to my opinion in this matter, which is as honest as it is strict, I would like to impart one more clause of my moral code against *vice*: with the word vice I combat every sort of anti-nature or, if one likes beautiful words, idealism. The clause reads: 'The preaching

46

of chastity is a public incitement to anti-nature. Every expression of contempt for the sexual life, every befouling of it through the concept "impure", is *the* crime against life – is the intrinsic sin against the holy spirit of life.'

6

To give an idea of me as a psychologist I take a curious piece of psychology which occurs in 'Beyond Good and Evil' – I forbid, by the way, any conjecture as to whom I am describing in this passage: 'The genius of the heart as it is possessed by that great hidden one, the tempter god and born pied piper of consciences whose voice knows how to descend into the underworld of every soul, who says no word and gives no glance in which there lies no touch of enticement, to whose mastery belongs knowing how to seem – not what he is but what to those who follow him is one constraint *more* to press ever closer to him, to follow him ever more inwardly and thoroughly . . . The genius of the heart who makes everything loud and self-satisfied fall silent and teaches it to listen, who smooths rough souls and gives them a new desire to savour – the desire to lie still as a mirror, that the deep sky may mirror itself in them . . . The genius of the heart who teaches the stupid and hasty hand to hesitate and grasp more delicately; who divines the hidden and forgotten treasure, the drop of goodness and sweet spirituality under thick and opaque ice, and is a divining-rod for every grain of gold which has lain long in the prison of much mud and sand . . . The genius of the heart from whose touch everyone goes away richer, not favoured and surprised, not as if blessed and oppressed with the goods of others, but richer in himself, newer to himself than before, broken open, blown upon and sounded out by a thawing wind, more uncertain perhaps, more delicate, more fragile, more broken, but full of hopes that as yet have no names, full of new will and current, full of new ill will and counter current . . .'

THE BIRTH OF TRAGEDY

I

IN order to be just to 'The Birth of Tragedy' (1872) one will have to forget a few things. It made its *effect* and even exercised fascination through what was wrong with it – through its application to *Wagnerism*, as if this were a symptom of a *beginning*. That is what made this book an event in Wagner's life: it was only from then on that great hopes surrounded the name Wagner. Even today people remind me, sometimes in the middle of Parsifal, that it is really *I* who have it on my conscience that so high an opinion of the *cultural value* of this movement has come to predominate. – I have often found the book cited as 'the Rebirth of Tragedy out of the Spirit of Music': people have had ears only for a new formula for the art, the intention, the task of *Wagner* – what of value was concealed in the book was thereby not listened to. 'Hellenism and Pessimism': that would have been a less ambiguous title: that is to say as a first instruction in how the Greeks got rid of pessimism – with what they *overcame* it . . . Precisely tragedy is the proof that the Greeks were *no* pessimists: Schopenhauer blundered in this as he blundered in everything. – Taken up and viewed impartially, 'The Birth of Tragedy' looks very untimely: one would not dream it was *begun* amid the thunders of the battle of Wörth. I thought these problems through before the walls of Metz, in cold September nights while serving in the medical corps; one would rather believe the book to be fifty years older. It is politically indifferent – 'un-German' one would say today – it smells offensively Hegelian, it is in only a few formulas infected with the cadaverous perfume of

Schopenhauer. An 'idea' – the antithesis Dionysian and Apollonian – translated into the metaphysical; history itself as the evolution of this 'idea'; in tragedy this antithesis elevated to a unity; from this perspective things which had never before caught sight of one another suddenly confronted with one another, illuminated by one another and *comprehended* . . . for example opera and revolution . . . The book's two decisive *novelties* are, firstly the understanding of the *dionysian* phenomenon in the case of the Greeks – it offers the first psychology of this phenomenon, it sees in it the sole root of the whole of Hellenic art –. The other novelty is the understanding of Socratism: Socrates for the first time recognized as an agent of Hellenic disintegration, as a typical *décadent*. 'Rationality' *against* instinct. 'Rationality' at any price as dangerous, as a force undermining life! – A profound hostile silence with regard to Christianity throughout the book. Christianity is neither Apollonian nor Dionysian, it *negates* all *aesthetic* values – the only values 'The Birth of Tragedy' recognizes: it is in the profoundest sense nihilistic, while in the Dionysian symbol there is attained the extreme limit of *affirmation*. In one place the Christian priests are alluded to as a 'malicious species of dwarfs', as 'subterraneans' . . .

2

This beginning is remarkable beyond all measure. I had *discovered* the only likeness and parallel to my own innermost experience which history possesses – I had therewith become the first to comprehend the wonderful phenomenon of the dionysian. By recognizing Socrates as a *décadent* I likewise offered a quite unambiguous proof of how little the certainty of my psychological grasp stood in danger of influence from any kind of moral idiosyncrasy – morality itself as a symptom of *décadence* is a novelty, a unique event of the first order in the history of knowledge. How high above and far beyond the pitiable shallow-pated chatter about optimism *contra* pessimism I had leapt with these conceptions! – I was the first to see the real antithesis – the *degenerated* instinct which turns against life with subterranean vengefulness (– Christianity, the philosophy of Schopenhauer, in a certain sense already the philosophy of Plato, the whole of idealism as typical forms) and a formula of *supreme affirmation* born out of fullness, of superfluity, an affirmation without reservation even of suffering, even of guilt, even of all that is strange and questionable in existence . . . This ultimate, joyfullest, boundlessly exuberant Yes to life is not only the highest insight, it is also the *profoundest*, the insight most strictly confirmed and maintained by truth and knowledge. Nothing that is can be subtracted, nothing is dispensable – the sides of existence rejected by Christians and other nihilists are even of endlessly higher rank in the order of rank of values than that which the *décadence* instinct may approve of and call good. To grasp this requires *courage* and, as a condition of this, a superfluity of *strength*: for precisely as far as courage *may* dare to go forward, precisely by this measure of strength does one approach truth. Recognition, affirmation of reality is for the strong man as great a necessity as is for the weak man, under the inspiration of weakness, cowardice and *flight* in the face of reality – the 'ideal' . . . They are not at liberty to know: *décadents need* the lie – it is one of the conditions of their existence. – He who not only understands the word 'dionysian' but understands *himself* in the word 'dionysian' needs no refutation of Plato or of Christianity or of Schopenhauer – *he smells the decomposition . . .*

3

The extent to which I therewith discovered the concept 'tragic', the knowledge at last attained of what the psychology of tragedy is, I most recently expressed in the *Twilight of the Idols*. 'Affirmation of life even in its strangest and sternest problems; the will to life rejoicing in its own inexhaustibility through the *sacrifice* of its highest types – *that* is what I called dionysian, that

is what I recognized as the bridge to the psychology of the *tragic* poet. *Not* so as to get rid of pity and terror, not so as to purify oneself of a dangerous emotion through its vehement discharge – it was thus Aristotle misunderstood it – : but, beyond pity and terror, *to realize in oneself* the eternal joy of becoming – the joy which also encompasses *joy in destruction . . .*'
In this sense I have the right to understand myself as the first *tragic philosopher* – that is to say the extremest antithesis and antipodes of a pessimistic philosopher. Before me this transposition of the dionysian into a philosophical pathos did not exist: *tragic wisdom* was lacking – I have sought in vain for signs of it even among the *great* Greeks of philosophy, those of the two centuries *before* Socrates. I retained a doubt in the case of *Heraclitus*, in whose vicinity in general I feel warmer and more well than anywhere else. Affirmation of transitoriness *and destruction*, the decisive element in a dionysian philosophy, affirmation of antithesis and war, *becoming* with a radical rejection even of the concept '*being*' – in this I must in any event recognize what is most closely related to me of anything that has been thought hitherto. The doctrine of 'eternal recurrence', that is to say of the unconditional and endlessly repeated circular course of all things – this doctrine of Zarathustra *could* possibly already have been taught by Heraclitus. At least the Stoa, which inherited almost all its fundamental ideas from Heraclitus, shows traces of it. –

4

A tremendous hope speaks out of this writing. I have in the end no reason whatever to renounce the hope for a dionysian future of music. Let us look a century ahead, let us suppose that my *attentat* on two millennia of anti-nature and the violation of man succeeds. That party of life which takes in hand the greatest of all tasks, the higher breeding of humanity, together with the remorseless destruction of all degenerate and parasitic elements, will again make possible on earth that *superfluity of life* out of which the dionysian condition must again proceed. I promise a *tragic age*: the supreme art in the affirmation of life, tragedy, will be reborn when mankind has behind it the consciousness of the harshest but most necessary wars *without suffering from it* ... A psychologist might add that what I in my youthful years heard in Wagnerian music had nothing at all to do with Wagner; that when I described dionysian music I described *that* which *I* had heard – that I had instinctively to translate and transfigure into the latest idiom all I bore within me. The proof of this, *as strong a proof as can be*, is my essay 'Wagner in Bayreuth': in all the psychologically decisive passages I am the only person referred to – one may ruthlessly insert my name or the word 'Zarathustra' wherever the text gives the word Wagner. The entire picture of the *dithyrambic* artist is a picture of the *pre-existent* poet of Zarathustra, sketched out with abysmal profundity and without so much as touching on the Wagnerian reality for a moment. Wagner himself had an idea of this: he failed to recognize himself in the essay. – The 'Bayreuth idea' had likewise transformed itself into something that those who know my Zarathustra will find no riddle: into that *great noontide* when the most select dedicate themselves to the greatest of all tasks – who knows? the vision of a festival I shall yet live to see ... The pathos of the first pages is world-historic; the *glance* which is spoken of is the actual glance of Zarathustra; Wagner, Bayreuth, the whole petty German wretchedness, is a cloud in which an endless *fata morgana* of the future is reflected. Even psychologically all the decisive traits of my own nature are worked into that of Wagner – the proximity to one another of the brightest and most fateful forces, the will to power as it has never been possessed by any man, the ruthless bravery in the things of the spirit, the boundless strength to learn without the will to action being thereby stifled. Everything in this essay is prophetic: the proximity of the return of the Greek spirit, the necessity for *counter Alexanders* to *retie* the Gordian knot of Greek culture after it had been untied ... Listen to the world-historic accent with which the concept 'tragic disposition' is introduced: there are in this essay nothing but world-historic accents. This is the strangest 'objectivity' there can be: the absolute certainty of what I *am* projected itself on to any reality that chanced to appear – the truth about myself spoke out of a dreadful depth. The *style* of Zarathustra is described and anticipated with incisive certainty; and one will find nowhere a more magnificent expression for the Zarathustra *event*, the act of a tremendous purification and dedication of mankind.

THE UNTIMELY ESSAYS

I

THE four *untimely essays* are altogether warlike. They demonstrate that I was no 'Jack o' Dreams', that I derive pleasure from drawing the sword – also, perhaps, that I have a dangerously supple wrist. The *first* attack (1873) was on German culture, which even at that time I already looked down on with remorseless contempt. Without meaning, without substance, without aim: a mere 'public opinion'. There is no more vicious misunderstanding than to believe that the Germans' great success in arms could demonstrate anything in favour of this culture – not to speak of *its* victory over France ... The *second* untimely essay (1874) brings to light what is dangerous, what gnaws at and poisons life, in our way of carrying on science –: life *sick* with this inhuman clockwork and mechanism, with the '*im*personality' of the worker, with the false economy of 'division of labour'. The *goal* gets lost, culture – the means, the modern way of carrying on science, *barbarized* ... In this essay the 'historical sense' of which this century is so proud is recognized for the first time as a sickness, as a typical sign of decay. – In the *third* and *fourth* untimely essays two pictures of the sternest *selfishness, self-discipline* are erected against this, as signposts to a *higher* concept of culture, to the restoration of the concept 'culture': untimely types *par excellence*, full of sovereign contempt for all that around them which was called 'Reich', 'culture', 'Christianity', 'Bismarck', 'success' – Schopenhauer and Wagner *or*, in *one* word, Nietzsche ...

2

Of these four *attentats*, the first enjoyed an extraordinary success. The noise it called forth was in every sense magnificent. I had touched a victorious nation on its sore spot – that its victory was *not* a cultural event, but perhaps, perhaps something quite different ... The reply came from all sides and by no means merely from old friends of David Strauss, whom I had rendered ludicrous as the type of a German culture-philistine and *satisfait*, in short as the author of an ale-house gospel of 'old faith and new' (– the word culture-philistine [*Bildungsphilister*] has remained in the language from its employment in my essay). These old friends, whom as Würthembergers and Swabians I had cut to the quick when I found their prodigy, their Strauss comical, replied as staunchly and uncouthly as I could possibly have wished; the Prussian retorts were cleverer – they had more 'Berlin blue' in them. The most indecent came from a Leipzig paper, the infamous 'Grenzboten'; I had trouble restraining the enraged Baselers from taking steps against it. The only people unconditionally on my side were a number of elderly gentlemen and their motives were mixed and in part undiscoverable. Among them Ewald of Göttingen, who gave it out that my *attentat* had proved fatal to Strauss. Likewise the old Hegelian Bruno Bauer, in whom I have from then on had one of my most attentive readers. In his last years he liked to refer for example Heinrich von Treitschke, the Prussian historiographer, to me for a hint as to where he might find information about the concept 'culture' which he had lost hold of. The most thoughtful, also the longest commentary on the essay and its author was uttered by a former pupil of the philosopher von Baader, a Professor Hoffmann of Würzburg. He foresaw from this essay a great vocation for me – to bring about a kind of crisis and supreme decision in the problem of atheism, the most instinctive and ruthless advocate of which he divined me to be. It was atheism which led me to Schopenhauer. – By far the best heard and most bitterly felt reaction was an extraordinarily strong and courageous defence by the usually so moderate Karl Hillebrand, that last *humane* German who knew how to wield the pen. His essay appeared in the 'Augsburger Zeitung'; it is included in a somewhat more cautious form in his collected writings. Here my essay was represented as an event, a turning-point, a first calling of oneself to order, as the best of all signs, as a real *return* of German seriousness and German passion in spiritual things. Hillebrand was full of high regard for the form of the essay, for its mature taste, for its perfect tact in distinguishing between the person and the matter at issue: he designated it the finest polemical writing to be written in German – in the art of polemics so dangerous and inadvisable for Germans. Unconditionally affirmative, even more severe than I had ventured to be on the ruination of language going on in Germany (– today they play the purist and can no longer construct a sentence –), equally contemptuous of the 'leading writers' of this nation, he ended by expressing his admiration for my *courage* – that 'supreme courage which calls the favourites of a nation to account' . . . The after-effect of this essay has been downright inestimable in my life. Up to now no one has sought to quarrel with me. One keeps silent, one treats me in Germany with a gloomy caution: I have for years employed an unconditional freedom of speech for which no one today, least of all in Germany, has his *hand* sufficiently free. My paradise is 'beneath the shadow of my sword' . . . What I really did was to put into practice a maxim of Stendhal's: he advised one to make one's entry into society with a *duel*. And how well I had chosen my opponent! the foremost German freethinker! . . . In fact it was a quite *new* kind of freethinking which therewith first found expression: to the present day there is nothing more foreign or unrelated to me than the entire European and American species of *'libres penseurs'*. I even feel myself more deeply divided from these incorrigible shallow-pates and buffoons of 'modern ideas' than I do from any of their opponents. They too want in their own way to 'improve' mankind, after their image, they would wage an implacable war against what I am, what I *want*, if they understood it – they one and all still believe in the 'ideal' ... I am the first *immoralist* –

3

That the untimely essays designated with the names Schopenhauer and Wagner could contribute very greatly to an understanding of these two cases, or even to the posing of psychological questions about them, I would not like to assert – a few things in them of course excepted. Thus, for example, what is elemental in Wagner's nature is even here with profound certainty of instinct designated as an actor's talent the methods and objectives of which are only consequences of it. What I really wanted to do in these essays was something quite other than to pursue psychology – a problem of education without its like, a new concept of *self-discipline*, *self-defence* to the point of harshness, a way to greatness and to world-historical tasks demanded its first expression. What I did by and large was to take two famous and still altogether undetermined types by the forelock, as one takes an opportunity by the forelock, in order to say something, in order to have a couple more formulas, signs, means of expression in my hands. This is, with perfectly uncanny sagacity, even indicated in the third untimely essay. It was in this way that Plato employed Socrates, as a semiotic for Plato. – Now, when I look back from a distance at the circumstances of which these essays are a witness, I would not wish to deny that fundamentally they speak only of me. The essay 'Wagner in Bayreuth' is a vision of my future; on the other hand, in 'Schopenhauer as Educator' it is my innermost history, my *evolution* that is inscribed. Above all my *solemn vow*! ... What I am today, *where* I am today – at a height at which I no longer speak with words but with lightning-bolts – oh how far away I was from it in those days! – But I *saw* the land – I did not deceive myself for a moment as to the way, sea, danger – *and* success! Great repose in promising, this happy looking outward into a future which shall not always remain a promise!

– Here every word is experienced, profound, inward; the most painful things are not lacking, there are words in it which are downright bloodsoaked. But a wind of the *great* freedom blows across everything; the wound itself does *not* act as an objection. – How I understand the philosopher, as a fearful explosive material from which everything is in danger, how I remove my concept 'philosopher' miles away from a concept which includes in it even a Kant, not to speak of the academic 'ruminants' and other professors of philosophy: as to this the essay offers an invaluable instruction, even admitting that what is being spoken of is fundamentally not 'Schopenhauer as Educator' but his *opposite*, 'Nietzsche as Educator'. – Considering that my trade was at this time that of a scholar, and perhaps too that I *understood* my trade, an astringent piece of psychology of the scholar which suddenly appears in this essay is not without significance: it expresses *feeling of distance*, my profound certainty as to what can be my *task* and what merely means, interlude and extra. It is my sagacity to have been many things and in many places so as to be able to become *one person* – so as to be able to attain *one thing*. For a time I *had* also to be a scholar. –

HUMAN, ALL TOO HUMAN
With Two Supplements

—

I

'HUMAN, All Too Human' is the memorial of a crisis. It calls itself a book for *free* spirits: almost every sentence in it is the expression of a victory – with this book I liberated myself from that in my nature which *did not belong to me*. Idealism does not belong to me: the title says: 'where *you* see ideal things, *I* see – human, alas all too human things!' . . . I know humanity *better* . . . The expression 'free spirit' should here be understood in no other sense: a spirit that has *become free*, that has again seized possession of itself. The tone, the sound of the voice has completely changed: one will find the book sagacious, cool, sometimes harsh and mocking. A certain spirituality of *noble* taste seems to be in constant struggle to keep itself aloft above a more passionate current running underneath. In this connection there is significance in the fact that it is actually the hundredth anniversary of the death of Voltaire with which the book as it were apologizes for being published in 1878. For Voltaire is, in contrast to all who have written after him, above all a *grandseigneur* of the spirit: precisely what I am too. – The name of Voltaire on a writing by me – that really was progress – *towards myself* . . . If one looks more closely, one discovers a merciless spirit who knows every hiding-place in which the ideal is at home – where it has its castle-keep and as it were its last place of security. With a torch in hand which gives no trembling light I illuminate with piercing brightness this *under-world* of the ideal. It is a war, but a war without powder and smoke, without warlike attitudes, without pathos and contorted limbs – all this would still have been 'idealism'. One error after

another is calmly laid on ice, the ideal is not refuted – *it freezes*
... Here for example 'the genius' freezes; on the next corner
'the saint' freezes; 'the hero' freezes into a thick icicle; at last
'faith', so-called 'conviction', freezes; 'pity' also grows consider-
ably cooler – almost everywhere 'the thing in itself' freezes ...

2

The beginnings of this book belong within the weeks of the
first Bayreuth Festival; a profound estrangement from all that
surrounded me there is one of its preconditions. Anyone who
has any idea what visions had been flitting across my path even
at that time can guess how I felt when I one day came to myself
in Bayreuth. It was as if I had been dreaming ... Where was I?
I recognized nothing, I hardly recognized Wagner. In vain I
scanned my memories. Tribschen – a distant isle of the blessed:
not the shadow of a resemblance. The incomparable days of the
foundation-stone laying, the little band of *initiates* who celebrated them and who did not lack fingers for delicate things:
not the shadow of a resemblance. *What had happened*? – Wagner
had been translated into German! The Wagnerian had become
master of Wagner! – *German* art! The *German* master! *German*
beer! ... We others, who know only too well to how refined a
species of artists, to how cosmopolitan a taste Wagner's art
alone speaks, were beside ourselves to rediscover Wagner be-
decked with German 'virtue'. – I think I know the Wagnerian,
I have 'experienced' three generations of them, from the late
Brendel, who confused Wagner with Hegel, to the 'idealists' of
the Bayreuther Blätter, who confuse Wagner with themselves –
I have heard every kind of confession about Wagner from
'beautiful souls'. A kingdom for *one* sensible word! – Truly, a
hair-raising crowd! Nohl, Pohl, *Kohl* charmingly *in infinitum*!
Not an abortion was missing, not even the anti-Semite. – Poor
Wagner! To what a pass had he come! – Better for him to have
gone among swine! But among Germans! ... For the instruction of posterity a genuine Bayreuther ought in the end to be

stuffed, better still preserved in spirit, for spirit is what is lacking – with the inscription: this is what the 'spirit' was like upon which the 'Reich' was founded ... Enough, I left in the midst of this for a couple of weeks, very suddenly, even though a charming Parisienne tried to console me; I excused myself to Wagner merely with a fatalistic telegram. At a place deeply buried in the Bohemian Forest, Klingenbrunn, I bore my melancholy and contempt for Germans about with me like an illness – *and* wrote a sentence in my pocket-book from time to time under the general title 'The Ploughshare', nothing but *hard* psychologica which can perhaps still be rediscovered in 'Human, All Too Human'.

3

What then resolved itself within me was not merely a breach with Wagner – I sensed a total aberration of my instinct of which the individual blunder, call it Wagner or my professorship at Basel, was merely a sign. I was overcome with *impatience* at myself; I realized it was high time for me to think back to *myself*. It became of a sudden terribly clear to me how much time I had already squandered – how useless, how capricious my whole philologist's existence appeared when compared with my task. I was ashamed of this *false* modesty ... Ten years behind me during which the *nourishment* of my spirit had quite literally been at a stop, during which I had learned nothing useful, during which I had forgotten inordinately much over a trash of dusty scholarship. Creeping meticulously and with bad eyesight through antique metrists – that is what I had come to! – I was moved to compassion when I saw myself quite thin, quite wasted away: *realities* were altogether lacking in my knowledge, and the 'idealities' were worth damn all! – A downright burning thirst seized hold of me: thenceforward I pursued in fact nothing other than physiology, medicine and natural science – I returned to actual historical studies only when the *task* imperiously compelled me to. It was then too that I first divined the connection between an activity chosen contrary to one's instincts, a so-called 'calling' to which one is called *least of all* – and that need for a *stupefaction* of the feeling of emptiness and hunger through a narcotic art – for example through Wagnerian art. A more careful survey has revealed to me that a large number of young men are in a like predicament: one piece of anti-nature downright *compels* a second. In Germany, in the 'Reich', to speak without ambiguity, all too many are condemned to decide too soon and then to *sicken away* beneath a burden they find they cannot throw off . . . Such people desire Wagner as an *opiate* – they forget themselves, they are free of themselves for a moment . . . What am I saying? *for five or six hours!* –

4

At that time my instinct decided inexorably against any further giving way, going along, confounding of myself with what I was not. Any kind of life, the most unfavourable conditions, sickness, poverty – all seemed preferable to that unworthy 'selflessness' into which I had first got out of ignorance, out of *youth*, in which I had subsequently remained out of lethargy, out of so-called 'sense of duty'. – Here there came to my aid, in a way I cannot sufficiently admire and at precisely the right time, that *bad* inheritance from my father's side – fundamentally a predestination to an early death. Sickness *liberated me slowly*: it spared me any kind of breach, any violent or offensive step. I forfeited no goodwill at that time and gained much. Sickness likewise gave me a right to a complete reversal of my habits; it permitted, it *commanded* forgetting; it bestowed on me the *compulsion* to lie still, to be idle, to wait and be patient . . . But to do that means to think! . . . My eyes alone put an end to all bookwormishness, in plain terms philology: I was redeemed from the 'book', for years at a time I read nothing – the *greatest* favour I have ever done myself! – That deepest self, as it were buried and grown silent under a constant *compulsion to listen* to other selves (— and that is what reading means!) awoke slowly, timidly, doubtfully — but at length it *spoke again*. I have never been so happy with myself as in the sickest and most painful periods of my life: one has only to look at 'Daybreak' or perhaps the 'Wanderer and his Shadow' to grasp what this 'return to *myself*' was: a highest kind of *recovery* itself! ... The other kind merely followed from this. —

5

Human, All Too Human, this memorial of a rigorous self-discipline with which I made a sudden end of every sort of 'higher swindle', 'idealism', 'beautiful feelings' and other woman-ishnesses that I had been infected with, was written chiefly in Sorrento; it received its conclusion, its final form during a Basel winter under far less favourable conditions than those in Sorrento. It is really Herr *Peter Gast*, then studying in Basel and very attached to me, who has the book on his conscience. I dictated, my head bandaged and painful, he wrote, he also corrected — he was really the actual writer, while I was merely the author. When the book finally arrived finished into my hands — to the profound astonishment of a serious invalid — I sent among others two copies to Bayreuth. Through a miracle of meaningful chance I received at the same time a beautiful copy of the Parsifal text, with Wagner's dedication to me, 'his dear friend Friedrich Nietzsche, Richard Wagner, Ecclesiastical Counsellor'. — This crossing of the two books — it seemed to me to make an ominous sound. Was it not as though two *swords* had crossed? ... At least we both felt it to be so: for we both kept silent. — About this time the first Bayreuther Blätter appeared: I grasped *for what* it had been high time. — Incredible! Wagner had become pious ...

6

What I thought about myself at that time (1876), with what tremendous certainty I held in my hands my task and what was world-historic in it, the whole book, but especially a very explicit passage, bears witness: except that, with my instinctive cunning, I here too avoided the little word 'I', and this time it was not Schopenhauer or Wagner but one of my friends, the excellent Dr Paul Rée, whom I bathed in world-historic glory – who was happily far too refined a creature to ... *Others* were less refined: I have always recognized the hopeless cases among my readers, the typical German professor for example, in that they have on the basis of this passage believed themselves compelled to understand the whole book as higher réealism ... In fact it contains a contradiction of five or six propositions of my friend: a point discussed in the preface to the 'Genealogy of Morals'. – The passage reads: But what is the main proposition arrived at by one of the boldest and coldest of thinkers, the author of the book 'On the Origin of the Moral Sensations' (*lisez*: Nietzsche, the first *immoralist*), by virtue of his incisive and penetrating analysis of human behaviour? 'Moral man is no closer to the intelligible world than physical man – *for* there is no intelligible world . . .' This proposition, hardened and sharpened beneath the hammer-blow of historical knowledge (*lisez*: Revaluation of All Values), may perhaps at some future time – 1890! – serve as the axe which is laid at the root of the 'metaphysical need' of man – whether more of a blessing or a curse to mankind who could say? But in any event as a proposition with the weightiest consequences, at once fruitful and fearful and looking out at the world with the *Janus-face* possessed by all great perceptions . . .

DAYBREAK
Thoughts about Morality as a Prejudice

I

WITH this book begins my campaign against *morality*. Not that it smells in the slightest of gunpowder – quite other and more pleasant odours will be perceived in it, provided one has some subtlety in one's nostrils. Neither big nor even small guns: if the effect of the book is negative, its means are all the less so, means from which the effect follows like a conclusion *not* like a cannon-shot. That one takes leave of the book with a cautious reserve in regard to everything that has hitherto been honoured and even worshipped under the name morality does not contradict the fact that in the entire book there is no negative word, no attack, no malice – that it rather lies in the sun, round, happy, like a sea-beast sunning itself among rocks. In the end it was I myself who was this sea-beast: almost every sentence in the book was thought, *tracked down* among that confusion of rocks near to Genoa where I was alone and still shared secrets with the sea. Even now, when I chance to light on this book every sentence becomes for me a spike with which I again draw something incomparable out of the depths: its entire skin trembles with tender shudders of recollection. The art in which it is preeminent is no small one in making things which easily slip by without a sound, moments which I call divine lizards, stay still for a little – not with the cruelty of that young Greek god who simply impaled the poor little lizard, but none the less still with something sharp, with the pen . . . 'There are so many daybreaks that have not yet dawned' – this *Indian* inscription stands on the gateway to this book. Where does its author *seek* that new dawn, that hitherto still undetected tender roseate sky with which another day – ah, a whole series, a whole world of new days! – breaks? In a *revaluation of all values*, in an escape from all moral values, in an affirmation of and trust in all that has hitherto been forbidden, despised, accursed. This *affirmative* book pours its light, its love, its tenderness upon nothing but evil things, it restores to them their 'soul', the good conscience, the exalted right and *privilege* to exist. Morality is not attacked, it only no longer comes into consideration . . . This book ends with an 'Or?' – it is the only book which ends with an 'Or?' . . .

2

My task, to prepare a moment of supreme coming-to-oneself on the part of mankind, a *great noontide* when it looks back and looks forward, when it steps out from the dominion of chance and the priesthood and poses the question why? to what end? for the first time as a *whole* – this task follows of necessity from the insight that mankind is *not* of itself on the right path, that it is absolutely *not* divinely directed, that under precisely its holiest value-concepts rather the instinct of denial, of decay, the *décadence* instinct has seductively ruled. The question of the origin of moral values is therefore for me a question of the *first rank* because it conditions the future of mankind. The demand that one ought to *believe* that fundamentally everything is in the best hands, that a book, the Bible, will set one's mind finally at rest as to divine governance and wisdom in the destiny of mankind, is translated back into reality, the will to suppress the truth as to the pitiable opposite of this, namely that hitherto mankind has been in the *worst* hands, that it has been directed by the under-privileged, the cunningly revengeful, the so-called 'saints', those world-calumniators and desecraters of man. The decisive sign that reveals that the priest (– including the *concealed* priest, the philosopher) has become master not only within a certain religious community but in general is that *décadence* morality, the will to the end, counts as morality *in itself*, is the unconditional value everywhere accorded to the unegoistic and the hostility accorded the egoistic. Whoever does not agree with me on this point I consider *infected* . . . But the whole world does not agree with me . . . For a physiologist such a value-antithesis admits of no dubiety. When within an organism the meanest organ neglects even to the slightest degree to assert with absolute certainty its self-preservation, indemnity for its expenditure of force, its 'egoism', the whole degenerates. The physiologist demands *excision* of the degenerate part, he denies any solidarity with it, he is far from pitying it. But the priest *wants* precisely the degeneration of the whole, of mankind: that is why he *conserves* the degenerate part – at this price he dominates mankind . . . What is the purpose of those lying concepts, the *ancillary* concepts of morality 'soul', 'spirit', 'free will', 'God', if it is not the physiological ruination of mankind? . . . When one directs seriousness away from self-preservation, enhancement of bodily strength, when one makes of greensickness an ideal, of contempt for the body 'salvation of the soul', what else is it but a *recipe for décadence*? – Loss of centre of gravity, resistance to the natural instincts, in a word 'selflessness' – that has hitherto been called *morality* . . . With 'Daybreak' I first took up the struggle against the morality of unselfing. –

THE GAY SCIENCE

'DAYBREAK' is an affirmative book, profound but bright and benevolent. The same applies once again and in the highest degree to the *gaya scienza*: in practically every sentence of this book profundity and exuberance go hand in hand. A poem which expresses gratitude for the most wonderful month of January I have ever experienced – the entire book is a gift – betrays out of what a depth 'science' has here become *gay*:

> You who with your spear of fire
> Melt the river of my soul,
> So that, freed from ice, it rushes
> Toward the ocean of its goal:
> Brighter still and still more healthy,
> Free in most desired constraint –
> Thus your miracle it praises,
> January, lovely saint!

As to what is here called 'goal' – who can be in any doubt as to what this means who sees glittering at the conclusion of the fourth book the diamond beauty of the opening words of Zarathustra? – Or who reads at the end of the third book the granite sentences with which a destiny for *all ages* formulates itself for the first time. – Songs of Prince Vogelfrei, composed for the most part in Sicily, call to mind quite explicitly the Provençal concept of '*gaya scienza*', that union of *minstrel, knight and free-spirit* by which that marvellous early culture of the Provençals is distinguished from all ambiguous cultures; the last poem of all especially, '*to the Mistral*', an exuberant dance-song in which, if I may say so! I dance right over morality, is a perfect Provençalism. –

THUS SPOKE ZARATHUSTRA
A Book for Everyone and No One

I

I SHALL now tell the story of Zarathustra. The basic conception of the work, the *idea of eternal recurrence*, the highest formula of affirmation that can possibly be attained – belongs to the August of the year 1881: it was jotted down on a piece of paper with the inscription: '6,000 feet beyond man and time'. I was that day walking through the woods beside the lake of Silvaplana; I stopped beside a mighty pyramidal block of stone which reared itself up not far from Surlei. Then this idea came to me. – If I reckon a couple of months back from this day I find as an omen a sudden and profoundly decisive alteration in my taste, above all in music. The whole of Zarathustra might perhaps be reckoned as music; – certainly a rebirth of the art of *hearing* was a precondition of it. In a little mountain resort not far from Vicenza, Recoaro, where I spent the spring of the year 1881, I discovered together with my *maestro* and friend Peter Gast, who was likewise 'reborn', that the phoenix music flew past us with lighter and more luminous wings than it had ever exhibited before. If on the other hand I reckon from that day forwards to the sudden delivery accomplished under the most improbable circumstances in February 1883 – the closing section, from which I have quoted a couple of sentences in the *Foreword*, was completed precisely at that sacred hour when Richard Wagner died in Venice – the pregnancy is seen to have lasted eighteen months. This term of precisely eighteen months might suggest, at least to Buddhists, that I am really a female elephant. – The interval is occupied by the '*gaya scienza*', which bears a hundred signs of the proximity of something incomparable;

finally it gives the opening of Zarathustra itself, it gives in the penultimate piece of the fourth book the fundamental idea of Zarathustra. – Also belonging to this interval is that *Hymn to Life* (for mixed chorus and orchestra) the score of which was published two years ago by E. W. Fritzsch of Leipzig: a perhaps not insignificant symptom of the condition of this year, when I was possessed to the highest degree by the *affirmative* pathos *par excellence*, which I call the tragic pathos. It will one day be sung to my memory. – The text, I may state expressly because a misunderstanding exists about it, is not by me: it is the astonishing inspiration of a young Russian lady with whom I was then friendly, Fräulein Lou von Salomé. He who knows how to extract any meaning at all from the closing words of the poem will divine why I preferred and admired it: they possess greatness. Pain does *not* count as an objection to life: 'Have you no more happiness to give me, well then! *still do you have your pain ...' Perhaps my music is also great at this point.* [*Last note* of the clarinet in A is *C sharp* not *C*. Printing error.) – I lived the following winter in the pleasantly quiet bay of Rapallo not far from Genoa which cuts in between Chiavari and the promontory of Porto Fino. My health was not of the best; the winter cold and exceedingly wet; a small *albergo* situated right against the sea, so that at night the high tide made sleep impossible, offered all in all the very opposite of what one might desire. In spite of this, and almost as a proof of my proposition that everything decisive comes about 'in spite of', it was during this winter and under these unfavourable conditions that my Zarathustra came into existence. – In the mornings I climbed in a southerly direction into the heights along the glorious route to Zoagli, past pine-trees and with a vast view of the sea; in the afternoons, whenever my health permitted I walked around the entire bay from Santa Margherita to Porto Fino. This place and this landscape is even closer to my heart through the great love Kaiser Friedrich the Third felt for it; in the autumn of 1886 I happened to be on this coast again when he visited this little forgotten world of happiness for the last time. – It was on these two walks that the whole of the first Zarathustra came to me, above all Zarathustra himself, as a type: more accurately, *he stole up on me* . . .

2

To understand this type one has first to become clear as to its physiological presupposition: it is that which I call *great health*. I do not know how to illustrate this conception better or *more personally* than I have already done in one of the last sections of the fifth book of the '*gaya scienza*'. 'We new, name-less, ill-understood' – it says there – 'we premature-born of a yet undemonstrated future, we need for a new goal also a new means, namely a new health, a stronger, shrewder, tougher, more daring, more cheerful health than any has been hitherto. He whose soul thirsts to have experienced the whole compass of values and desiderata and to have sailed around every coast of this "Middle Sea" of ideals, who wants to know from the adventures of his own most personal experience how a con-queror and discoverer of the ideal feels, likewise how an artist, a saint, a lawgiver, a sage, a scholar, a man of piety, a divine hermit of the old stamp feels: he needs one thing before all else, *great health* – a health such as one does not merely have but has continually to win because one has again and again to sacrifice it . . . And now, after having been thus under way for a long time, we Argonauts of the ideal, braver perhaps than is prudent and often enough shipwrecked and come to grief but, as said, healthier than others would like us to be, dangerously healthy, healthy again and again – it seems to us as if we have, as a reward, a yet undiscovered country before us whose boundaries none has ever seen, a land beyond all known lands and corners of the ideal, a world so overfull of the beautiful, strange, questionable, terrible and divine that our curiosity and our thirst for possession are both beside themselves so that nothing can any longer satisfy us! . . . How, after such prospects and with such a ravenous hunger in conscience and knowledge,

could we remain content with the *man of the present*? It is hard
enough to remain serious when we regard his worthiest hopes
and objectives, and perhaps we do not even regard them any
more ... Another ideal runs ahead of us, a strange, seductive,
dangerous ideal to which we do not want to convert anyone
because we do not easily admit that anyone has a *right to it*: the
ideal of a spirit who naively, that is to say impulsively and from
overflowing plenitude and power, plays with everything hitherto called holy, good, untouchable, divine; for whom the highest
things by which the people reasonably enough take their standards would signify something like a danger, a corruption, a
degradation, or at least a recreation, a blindness, a temporary
self-forgetfulness; the ideal of a human-super-human well-being
and well-wishing which will often enough seem *inhuman*, for
example when it is set beside the whole of earthly seriousness
hitherto, beside every kind of solemnity in gesture, word, tone,
glance, morality and task as their most corporal involuntary
parody – and with which, in spite of all that, perhaps *the great
seriousness* first arises, the real question-mark is first set up, the
destiny of the soul veers round, the clock-hand moves on, the
tragedy *begins* . . .'

3

– Has anyone at the end of the nineteenth century a distinct
conception of what poets of strong ages called *inspiration*? If
not, I will describe it. – If one had the slightest residue of
superstition left in one, one would hardly be able to set aside
the idea that one is merely incarnation, merely mouthpiece,
merely medium of overwhelming forces. The concept of revelation, in the sense that something suddenly, with unspeakable
certainty and subtlety, becomes *visible*, audible, something that
shakes and overturns one to the depths, simply describes the
fact. One hears, one does not seek; one takes, one does not ask
who gives; a thought flashes up like lightning, with necessity,
unfalteringly formed – I have never had any choice. An ecstasy

whose tremendous tension sometimes discharges itself in a flood of tears, while one's steps now involuntarily rush along, now involuntarily lag; a complete being outside of oneself with the distinct consciousness of a multitude of subtle shudders and trickles down to one's toes; a depth of happiness in which the most painful and gloomy things appear, not as an antithesis, but as conditioned, demanded, as a *necessary* colour within such a superfluity of light; an instinct for rhythmical relationships which spans forms of wide extent – length, the need for a *wide-spanned* rhythm is almost the measure of the force of inspiration, a kind of compensation for its pressure and tension . . . Everything is in the highest degree involuntary but takes place as in a tempest of a feeling of freedom, of absoluteness, of power, of divinity . . . The involuntary nature of image, of metaphor is the most remarkable thing of all; one no longer has any idea what is image, what metaphor, everything presents itself as the readiest, the truest, the simplest means of expression. It really does seem, to allude to a saying of Zarathustra's, as if the things themselves approached and offered themselves as metaphors (– 'here all things come caressingly to your discourse and flatter you: for they want to ride upon your back. Upon every image you here ride to every truth. Here, the words and word-chests of all existence spring open to you; all existence here wants to become words, all becoming here wants to learn speech from you –'). This is *my* experience of inspiration; I do not doubt that one has to go back thousands of years to find anyone who could say to me 'it is mine also'. –

4

I lay ill for a couple of weeks in Genoa. There followed a melancholy spring in Rome, where I merely put up with life – it was not easy. This place, the most improper in the world for the poet of Zarathustra and which I had not chosen voluntarily, vexed me beyond measure; I tried to get away – I wanted to go to *Aquila*, the counter-concept to Rome, founded out of enmity towards Rome, as I shall one day found a place to the memory of an atheist and enemy of the church *comme il faut*, to one who is most closely related to me, the great Hohenstaufen emperor Friedrich the Second. But a fatality hung over it all: I had to return. I finally acquiesced in the *piazza Barberini* after I had grown weary of trying to find an *anti-Christian* quarter. I am afraid that once, in an effort to escape the bad odours as much as possible, I asked at the *palazzo del Quirinale* itself whether they did not have a quiet room for a philosopher. – On a *loggia* high above the said *piazza*, from which one has a view across Rome and deep beneath the rustling of the *fontana* can be heard, that loneliest song was written that ever was written, the *Night Song*; at this time a melody of unspeakable melancholy went on continually around me whose refrain I rediscovered in the words 'dead of immortality . . .' In the summer, returned home to the sacred spot where the first lightning of the Zarathustra idea had flashed to me, I found the second Zarathustra. Ten days sufficed; in no case, neither with the first nor with the third and last did I require more. The following winter, beneath the halcyon sky of Nice, which then shone into my life for the first time, I found the third Zarathustra – and was done. The whole took hardly a year. Many hidden places and heights in the landscape of Nice are for me consecrated by unforgettable moments; that decisive chapter which bears the title 'Of Old and New Law-Tables' was composed during the most painful climb from the station to the marvellous Moorish hill castle Eza – my muscular agility has always been greatest when my creative power has flowed most abundantly. The *body* is inspired: let us leave the 'soul' out of it . . . I could often have been seen dancing; at that time I could walk for seven or eight hours in the mountains without a trace of tiredness. I slept well, I laughed a lot – I was perfectly vigorous and perfectly patient.

5

Apart from these ten-day works the years during and above all *after* Zarathustra were a state of distress without equal. One pays dearly for being immortal: one has to die several times while alive. — There is something I call the *rancune* of what is great: everything great, a work, a deed, once it is completed forthwith turns *against* him who did it. Precisely because he did it he is from then on *weak* – he can no longer endure his deed, he can no longer look it in the face. To have something *behind* one that one ought never to have willed, something within which the knot of destiny of mankind is tied – and from then on to have it *on* one! . . . It almost crushes . . . The *rancune* of what is great! – A second thing is the horrible silence one hears around one. Solitude has seven skins; nothing can get through them. One encounters people, one greets friends: new desolation, no glance offers a greeting. At best a kind of revolt. I experienced such a revolt, in very varying degrees but from almost everyone who was close to me; it seems that nothing gives greater offence than suddenly to let a distance become perceptible – *noble* natures who do not know how to live without venerating are rare. – A third thing is the absurd susceptibility of the skin to pinpricks, a kind of helplessness in the face of everything small. This seems to me to be conditioned by the tremendous expenditure of all defensive energies presupposed by every *creative* deed, every deed that comes from the most personal, innermost, deepest part of one's being. The *minor* defensive capabilities are thereby as it were suspended; they no longer receive any energy. – I also venture to suggest that one digests less well, prefers not to move, is all too vulnerable to feeling cold as well as mistrust – mistrust which is in many cases merely an etiological error. While in such a condition I once sensed the proximity of a herd of cows even before I saw them through the return of milder, more philanthropic thoughts: *that* had warmth in it . . .

6

This work stands altogether alone. Let us leave the poets aside: perhaps nothing at all has ever been done out of a like superfluity of strength. My concept 'dionysian' has here become the *supreme deed*; compared with it all the rest of human activity seems poor and conditional. That a Goethe, a Shakespeare would not for a moment have known how to breathe in this tremendous passion and solitude, that Dante is, compared with Zarathustra, merely a believer and not one who first *creates* truth, a *world-ruling* spirit, a destiny – that the poets of the Veda are priests and not even worthy to unloose the latchet of the shoes of a Zarathustra – all this is the least of it, and gives no idea of the distance, of the *azure* solitude, in which this work lives. Zarathustra has an eternal right to say: 'I form circles and holy boundaries around myself; fewer and fewer climb with me upon higher and higher mountains – I build a mountain range out of holier and holier mountains.' Reckon into a single sum the spirit and goodness of all great souls: all of them together would not be capable of producing one of Zarathustra's discourses. The ladder upon which he climbs up and down is tremendous; he has seen further, willed further, *been able* further than any other human being. He contradicts with every word, this most affirmative of all spirits; all opposites are in him bound together into a new unity. The highest and the lowest forces of human nature, the sweetest, most frivolous and most fearsome stream forth out of *one* fountain with immortal certainty. Until then one does not know what height, what depth is; one knows even less what truth is. There is no moment in this revelation of truth which would have been anticipated or divined by even *one* of the greatest. There is no wisdom, no psychology, no art of speech before Zarathustra: the nearest things, the most everyday things here speak of things unheard of. The aphorism trembling with passion; eloquence become music; lightning-bolts hurled ahead to hitherto undivined futures. The mightiest capacity for metaphor which has hitherto existed is poor and child's play compared with this return of language to the nature of imagery. – And how Zarathustra condescends and says the kindest things to everyone! How he takes even his opponents, the priests, with gentle hands and suffers from them with them! – Here man is overcome every moment, the concept 'superman' here becomes the greatest reality – all that has hitherto been called great in man lies at an infinite distance *beneath* it. The halcyon, light feet, the ubiquity of wickedness and exuberance and whatever else is typical of the type Zarathustra has never been dreamed of as essential to greatness. It is in precisely this compass of space, in this access to opposites that Zarathustra feels himself to be the *highest species of all existing things*, and when one hears how he defines this one will refrain from seeking what is like him.

— the soul which possesses the longest ladder and can descend the deepest,

the most spacious soul, which can run and stray and roam the farthest into itself,

the most necessary soul, which out of joy hurls itself into chance,

the existing soul which plunges into becoming, the possessing soul which *wants* to partake in desire and longing —

the soul fleeing from itself which retrieves itself in the widest sphere,

the wisest soul, to which foolishness speaks sweetest,

the soul that loves itself the most, in which all things have their current and counter-current and ebb and flow —

But that is the concept of Dionysos himself. — Another consideration leads to the same conclusion. The psychological problem in the type of Zarathustra is how he, who to an unheard-of degree says No, *does* No to everything to which one has hitherto said Yes, can none the less be the opposite of a spirit of denial; how he, a spirit bearing the heaviest of destinies, a fatality of a task, can none the less be the lightest and most opposite — Zarathustra is a dancer — : how he, who has the harshest, the most fearful insight into reality, who has thought the 'most abysmal thought', none the less finds in it no objection to existence, nor even to the eternal recurrence of existence — rather one more reason *to be himself* the eternal Yes to all things, 'the tremendous unbounded Yes and Amen' ... 'Into every abyss I still bear the blessing of my affirmation' ... *But that is the concept of Dionysos once more.*

7

– What language will such a spirit speak when he speaks with himself alone? The language of the *dithyramb*. I am the inventor of the dithyramb. Hear how Zarathustra speaks with himself *before sunrise*: such an emerald happiness, such a divine tenderness still had no tongue before me. Even the deepest melancholy of such a Dionysos still becomes a dithyramb; I take, as an indication, the *Night Song* – the immortal lament that through his superabundance of light and power, through his nature as a *sun*, he is condemned not to love.

It is night: now do all leaping fountains speak louder. And my soul too is a leaping fountain.

It is night: only now do all songs of lovers awaken. And my soul too is the song of a lover.

Something unquenched, unquenchable is in me, that wants to speak out. A craving for love is in me that itself speaks the language of love.

Light am I: ah, that I were night! But this is my solitude, that I am girded round with light.

Ah, that I were dark and obscure! How I would suck at the breasts of light!

And I should bless you, you little sparkling stars and glowworms above! – and be happy in your gifts of light.

But I live in my own light, I drink back into myself the flames that break from me.

I do not know the joy of the receiver; and I have often dreamed that stealing must be more blessed than receiving.

It is my poverty that my hand never rests from giving; it is my envy that I see expectant eyes and illumined nights of desire.

Oh wretchedness of all givers! Oh eclipse of my sun! Oh craving for desire! Oh ravenous hunger in satiety!

They take from me: but do I yet touch their souls? A gulf

stands between giving and receiving; and the smallest gulf must be bridged at last.

A hunger grows from out of my beauty: I should like to rob those to whom I give – thus do I hunger after wickedness.

Withdrawing my hand when another hand already reaches out to it; hesitating, like the waterfall that hesitates even in its plunge – thus do I hunger after wickedness.

Such vengeance does my abundance concoct: such spite wells from my solitude.

My joy in giving died in giving, my virtue grew weary of itself through its abundance!

The danger for him who always gives is that he may lose his shame; the hand and heart of him who distributes grow callous through sheer distributing.

My eye no longer overflows with the shame of suppliants; my hand has become too hard for the trembling of hands that have been filled.

Where have the tears of my eye and the bloom of my heart gone? Oh solitude of all givers! Oh silence of all light-givers

Many suns circle in empty space: to all that is dark they speak with their light – to me they are silent.

On, this is the enmity of light towards what gives light: unpitying it travels its way.

Unjust towards the light-giver in its inmost heart, cold towards suns – thus travels every sun.

Like a storm the suns fly along their courses; that is their travelling. They follow their inexorable will; that is their coldness.

Oh, it is only you, obscure, dark ones, who extract warmth from light-givers! Oh, only you drink milk and comfort from the udders of light!

Ah, ice is around me, my hand is burned with ice! Ah, thirst is in me, which yearns after your thirst!

It is night: ah, that I must be light! And thirst for the things of night! And solitude!

It is night: now my longing breaks from me like a well-spring – I long for speech.

It is night: now do all leaping fountains speak louder. And my soul too is a leaping fountain.

It is night: only now do all songs of lovers awaken. And my soul too is the song of a lover. –

8

The like of this has never been written, never felt, never *suffered*: thus does a god suffer, a Dionysos. The reply to such a dithyramb of a sun's solitude in light would be *Ariadne* . . . Who knows except me what *Ariadne* is! . . . Of all such riddles no one has hitherto had the solution, I doubt whether anyone even saw a riddle here. – On one occasion Zarathustra strictly defines his task – it is also mine – the *meaning* of which cannot be misunderstood: he is *affirmative* to the point of justifying, of redeeming even the entire past.

I walk among men as among fragments of the future: of that future which I scan.

And it is all my art and aim to compose into one and bring together what is fragment and riddle and dreadful chance.

And how could I endure to be a man, if man were not also poet and reader of riddles and the redeemer of chance!

To redeem the past and to transform every 'It was' into an 'I wanted it thus!' – that alone would I call redemption.

In another place he defines as strictly as possible what alone 'man' can be for him – *not* an object of love, not to speak of pity – Zarathustra has also mastered *great disgust* at man: to him man is formlessness, material, an ugly stone which requires the sculptor.

No more to *will* and no more to *evaluate* and no more to *create*! ah, that this great lassitude may ever stay far from me!

In knowing and understanding, too, I feel only my will's

delight in begetting and becoming; and if there be innocence in my knowledge it is because *will to begetting* is in it.

This will lured me away from God and gods; for what would there be to create if gods – existed!

But again and again it drives me to mankind, my ardent, creative will; thus it drives the hammer to the stone.

Ah you men, I see an image sleeping in the stone, the image of my visions! Ah, that it must sleep in the hardest, ugliest stone!

Now my hammer rages fiercely against its prison. Fragments fly from the stone: what is that to me?

I will complete it: for a shadow came to me – the most silent, the lightest of all things came to me!

The beauty of the superman came to me as a shadow: what are the gods to me now! . . .

I emphasize one final point: the italicized line provides the occasion. Among the decisive preconditions for a *dionysian* task is the hardness of the hammer, *joy even in destruction*. The imperative 'become hard', the deepest certainty *that all creators are hard*, is the actual mark of a dionysian nature. –

BEYOND GOOD AND EVIL
Prelude to a Philosophy of the Future

I

THE task for the immediately following years was as clear as it could be. Now that the affirmative part of my task was done, it was the turn of the denying, the No-saying and *No-doing* part: the revaluation of existing values themselves, the great war – the evocation of a day of decision. Included here is the slow search for those related to me, for such as out of strength would offer me their hand for *the work of destruction*. – From now on all my writings are fish-hooks: perhaps I understand fishing as well as anyone? . . . If nothing got *caught* I am not to blame. *There were no fish* . . .

2

This book (1886) is in all essentials a *critique of modernity*, the modern sciences, the modern arts, not even excluding modern politics, together with signposts to an antithetical type who is as little modern as possible, a noble, an affirmative type. In the latter sense the book is a *school for gentlemen*, that concept taken more spiritually *and radically* than it has ever been taken. One has to have courage in one even to endure it, one must never have learned fear . . . All the things of which the age is proud are felt as contradictions of this type, almost as bad manners, for example its celebrated 'objectivity', its 'sympathy with all that suffers', its 'historical sense' with its subjection to the taste of others, with its prostration before *petits faits*, its 'scientifical-ity'. – If one considers that the book comes *after* Zarathustra one will also perhaps divine the dietetic *regime* to which it owes its existence. The eye grown through a tremendous compulsion accustomed to seeing *afar* – Zarathustra is more farsighted even than the Tsar – is here constrained to focus sharply on what is close at hand, the age, what is *around us*. In every aspect of the book, above all in its form, one will discover the same *intentional* turning away from the instincts out of which a Zarathustra becomes possible. Refinement in form, in intention, in the art of *keeping silent*, is in the foreground, psychology is employed with an avowed harshness and cruelty – there is not a single good-natured word in the entire book ... All this is recuperative: who could in the end divine *what* kind of recuperation is needed after such an expenditure of goodness as Zarathustra is? ... Speaking theologically – pay heed, for I rarely speak as a theologian – it was God himself who at the end of his labour lay down as a serpent under the Tree of Knowledge: it was thus he recuperated from being God ... He had made everything too beautiful ... The Devil is merely the idleness of God on that seventh day ...

GENEALOGY OF MORALS
A Polemic

THE three essays of which this Genealogy consists are in regard to expression, intention and art of surprise perhaps the uncanniest things that have ever been written. Dionysos is, as one knows, also the god of darkness. – Each time a beginning which is *intended* to mislead, cool, scientific, even ironic, intentionally foreground, intentionally keeping in suspense. Gradually an increasing disquiet; isolated flashes of lightning; very unpleasant truths becoming audible as a dull rumbling in the distance – until at last a *tempo feroce* is attained in which everything surges forward with tremendous tension. At the conclusion each time amid perfectly awful detonations a *new* truth visible between thick clouds. – The truth of the *first* essay is the psychology of Christianity: the birth of Christianity out of the spirit of *ressentiment*, *not*, as is no doubt believed, out of the 'spirit' – essentially a counter-movement, the great revolt against the domination of *noble* values. The *second* essay gives the psychology of the *conscience*: it is *not*, as is no doubt believed, 'the voice of God in man' – it is the instinct of cruelty turned backwards after it can no longer discharge itself outwards. Cruelty here brought to light for the first time as one of the oldest substrata of culture and one that can least be thought away. The *third* essay gives the answer to the question where the tremendous *power* of the ascetic ideal, the priestly ideal, comes from, although it is the *harmful* ideal *par excellence*, a will to the end, a *décadence* ideal. Answer: *not* because God is active behind the priests, which is no doubt believed, but *faute de mieux* – because hitherto it has been the only ideal, because it had no competitors. 'For man will rather will nothingness than *not* will' ... What was lacking above all was a *counter-ideal* – *until the advent of Zarathustra*. – I have been understood. Three decisive preliminary studies of a psychologist for a revaluation of all values. – This book contains the first psychology of the priest.

TWILIGHT OF THE IDOLS
How to Philosophize with a Hammer

I

THIS writing of fewer than 150 pages, cheerful and fateful in tone, a demon which laughs – the work of so few days I hesitate to reveal their number, is the exception among books: there exists nothing more rich in substance, more independent, more overthrowing – more wicked. If you want to get a quick idea of how everything was upsidedown before me, make a start with this writing. That which is called *idol* on the title-page is quite simply that which has hitherto been called truth. *Twilight of the Idols* – in plain terms: the old truth is coming to an end . . .

2

There is no reality, no 'ideality' which is not touched on in this writing (– touched on: what a cautious euphemism! . . .). Not merely *eternal* idols, also the youngest of all, consequently weakest with age. 'Modern ideas', for example. A great wind blows among the trees and everywhere fruits fall – truths. There is the prodigality of an all too abundant autumn in it: one trips over truths, one even treads some to death – there are too many of them . . . But those one gets one's hands on are no longer anything questionable, they are decisions. Only I have the standard for 'truths' in my hand, only I *can* decide. As if in me a *second consciousness* had grown, as if in me 'the will' had turned on a light for itself over the *oblique* path on which it had hitherto been *descending* . . . The *oblique* path – it was called the 'path to truth' . . . All 'obscure impulse' is at an end, it is precisely the *good* man who has known least what was the right path ... And, in all seriousness, no one before me has known the right path, the *ascending* path: only after me are there again hopes, tasks, prescribable paths of culture – I *am the bringer of the good tidings of these* ... Precisely therewith am I a destiny. –

3

Immediately upon completing the said work and without losing so much as a day, I attacked the tremendous task of the Revaluation in a sovereign feeling of pride beyond compare, sure of my immortality every moment and engraving sign upon sign in brass tablets with the sureness of a destiny. The foreword was written on 3 September 1888: when in the morning after this writing I stepped outside I found awaiting me the loveliest day the Ober-Engadin had ever shown me – transparent, glowing in its colours, containing in itself every antithesis, every mediant between ice and south. – Only on 20 September did I leave Sils-Maria, detained there by floods, finally by far the last guest of this wonderful place to which my gratitude would like to make the gift of an immortal name. After a journey with incidents, even being in peril of my life in the flooded Como, which I reached only deep in the night, I arrived on the afternoon of the twenty-first in Turin, my *proved* place, my *Residenz* from now on. I took again the same accommodation I had occupied in the spring, *via Carlo Alberto 6, III*, opposite the mighty *palazzo Carignano*, in which *Vittorio Emanuele* was born, with a view of the *piazza Carlo Alberto* and beyond that to the hills. Without delay and without letting myself be distracted for a moment I resumed work: only the last quarter of the book remained to be done. On 30 September a great victory; seventh day; a god takes his leisure on the banks of the Po. On the same day I went on to write the *foreword* to the 'Twilight of the Idols', correction of the proofs of which had been my recreation during September. – I have never experienced such an autumn, nor have I thought anything of the sort possible on earth – a Claude Lorrain thought on to infinity, every day of the same excessive perfection. –

THE WAGNER CASE
A Musicians' Problem

I

IF one is to be fair to this writing one has to suffer from the destiny of music as from an open wound. – *What* is it I suffer from when I suffer from the destiny of music? From this: that music has been deprived of its world-transfiguring, affirmative character, that it is *décadence* music and no longer the flute of Dionysos ... Supposing, however, that one in this way feels the cause of music to be *one's own* cause, to be the history of *one's own* suffering, one will find this writing full of consideration and mild beyond measure. In such cases to be cheerful and good-naturedly to mock at oneself as well – *ridendo dicere severum* where *verum dicere* would justify every kind of severity – is humaneness itself. Who really doubts that I, old artillerist that I am, have the ability to bring up my *heavy* guns against Wagner? – I kept to myself everything decisive in this matter – I have loved Wagner. – Ultimately this is an attack on a subtle 'unknown' who could not easily be detected by another, in the sense and direction of my task – oh, I have still got quite other 'unknowns' to reveal than a Cagliostro of music – even more, to be sure, an attack on the German nation growing ever more sluggish and poor in instinct in spiritual matters, ever more *honourable*, which with an enviable appetite continues to nourish itself with opposites and knows how to gulp down 'faith' as well as scientificality, 'Christian love' as well as anti-Semitism, will to power (to the 'Reich') as well as the *évangile des humbles*, without having any trouble digesting them ... This lack of party in choosing between opposites! This ventral neutrality and 'selflessness'! This fairness of German *taste*, which accords

89

everything equal rights – which finds everything tasty ...
Without any doubt the Germans are idealists ... When I last
visited Germany I found German taste occupied in trying to
accord Wagner and the Trumpeter of Säckingen equal rights; I
myself witnessed how in Leipzig, to the honour of one of the
most genuine and German musicians in the old sense of the
word German, no mere Reich German, *Meister Heinrich Schütz*,
they founded a Liszt Society for the encouragement and propa-
gation of *cunning* church music ... Without any doubt the
Germans are idealists ...

2

But here nothing shall stop me from becoming rude and telling
the Germans a couple of hard truths: *who else will do it?* – I
speak of their indecency *in historicis*. German historians have
not only altogether lost the *grand view* for the course, for the
values of culture, and are one and all buffoons of politics (or of
the church –): they have even *outlawed* this grand view. One has
first of all to be 'German', to have 'race', then one can arbitrate
over all values and disvalues *in historicis* – one determines them
... 'German' is an argument, '*Deutschland, Deutschland über alles*'
a principle, the Germans represent the 'moral world-order' in
history; in relation to the *imperium romanum* the bearers of
freedom, in relation to the eighteenth century the restorers of
morality, of the 'categorical imperative' ... There is a *reichsdeutsch* historiography, there is, I am afraid, even an anti-Semitic
one – there is a *court* historiography and Herr von Treitschke is
not ashamed ... Recently an idiotic judgement *in historicis*, a
proposition of the happily late Swabian aesthetician Vischer,
went the rounds of the German newspapers as a 'truth' to
which every German *had to say Yes*: 'The Renaissance *and* the
Reformation, both together constitute a whole – the aesthetic
rebirth *and* the moral rebirth'. – In face of such propositions my
patience runs out, and I sense a desire, I feel it even to be a
duty, to tell the Germans for once *what* they already have on

their conscience. *Every great cultural crime of four centuries is what they have on their conscience*! ... And always from the same cause, from their most inherent *cowardice* in face of reality, which is also cowardice in face of truth, from the falseness which has become instinct with them, from 'idealism' ... The Germans deprived Europe of the seriousness, of the meaning of the last *great* age, the age of the Renaissance, at a moment when a higher order of values, when the noble, life-affirmative values which guarantee the future had achieved victory at the seat of the antithetical values, *the values of decline — and even into the instincts of him who sat on it*! Luther, that fatality of a monk, restored the church and, what is a thousand times worse, Christianity, at the moment *of its defeat* ... Christianity, that *denial of the will to life* become religion! ... Luther, who found it impossible to be a monk and who because of this 'impossibility' attacked the church and — consequently! — restored it ... Catholics would have reason to celebrate Luther Festivals, compose Luther plays ... Luther — and 'moral rebirth'! To the devil with all psychology! — Without doubt the Germans are idealists. — Twice, at precisely the moment when with tremendous courage and self-overcoming an honest, an unambiguous, a completely scientific mode of thinking had been attained, the Germans have known how to discover secret paths to the old 'ideal', reconciliations between truth and 'ideal', at bottom formulas for a right to reject science, for a right to *lie*. Leibniz and Kant — those two greatest impediments to the intellectual integrity of Europe! — Finally, when on the bridge between two *décadence* centuries a *force majeure* of genius and will became visible, strong enough to forge Europe into a political and *economic* unity for the purpose of ruling the earth, the Germans with their 'Wars of Liberation' deprived Europe of the meaning, of the miracle of meaning of the existence of Napoleon — they thereby have on their conscience everything that followed, that exists today, this sickness and unreason the *most inimical to culture* there is, nationalism, that *névrose nationale* with which Europe is sick, that eternalizing of the petty-state situation of

Europe, of *petty* politics: they have deprived Europe itself of its meaning, of its *reason* – they have led it into a blind alley. – Does anyone except me know a way out of this blind alley? . . . A task great enough once again to *unite* the peoples? . . .

3

– And why should I not in the end give expression to my suspicions? In my case too the Germans will again try everything to bring forth a mouse out of a tremendous destiny. Up to now they have compromised themselves with me, I doubt if they will do better in the future. – Ah, how I would like to be a *false* prophet in this instance! . . . The readers and auditors most natural to me are still Russians, Scandinavians and French – will they always be so? – In the history of knowledge the Germans are represented by nothing but ambiguous names, they have ever produced only 'unconscious' false-coiners (– Fichte, Schelling, Schopenhauer, Hegel, Schleiermacher deserve this description as well as Kant and Leibniz; they are all mere *Schleiermacher*, mere *veilmakers* –): they ought never to have the honour of harbouring the first *honest* spirit in the history of the spirit, the spirit in whom truth comes to judgement on the false-coinage of four millennia. The 'German spirit' is *my* bad air: I find it hard to breathe in the proximity of this uncleanliness *in psychologicis* become instinct which every word, every gesture of a German betrays. They never went through a seventeenth century of hard self-examination as the French did – a La Rochefoucauld, a Descartes is a hundred times superior in integrity to the leading Germans – to this day they have had no psychologists. But psychology is almost the measure of the *cleanliness* or *uncleanliness* of a race . . . And if one is not even clean how should one possess *depth*? With the German, almost as with the woman, one never gets to the bottom, *he has none*: that is all. But in that event one is not even shallow. – That which is in Germany called 'deep' is precisely this uncleanliness of instinct towards oneself of which I speak: one does not *want* to be clear about oneself. Might I not suggest the word 'German' as an international counter for *this* psychological depravity? – At this moment, for example, the German Kaiser calls it his 'Christian duty' to free the slaves in Africa: among us *other* Europeans let that be called simply 'German' . . . Have the Germans produced even one book that possessed profundity? They even lack any idea of what constitutes profundity in a book. I have known scholars who considered Kant profound; at the Prussian court, I fear, they consider Herr von Treitschke profound. And when I have occasionally praised Stendhal as a profound psychologist, it has happened to me that German university professors have asked me to spell his name . . .

<h1 style="text-align:center">4</h1>

– And why should I not go on to the end? I like to make a clean sweep. It is even part of my ambition to count as the despiser of the German *par excellence*. I expressed my *mistrust* of the German character already at the age of twenty-six (third untimely essay) – the Germans are impossible for me. Whenever I picture to myself a type of man that goes against all my instincts it always turns into a German. The first thing in which I 'test the reins' of a person is whether he has in him a feeling for distance, whether he sees everywhere rank, degree, order between man and man, whether he *distinguishes*: one is thereby a *gentleman*; in any other event one belongs irretrievably to the wide-hearted, alas! so good-hearted concept of the *canaille*. But the Germans are *canaille* – alas! they are so good-natured . . . One lowers oneself by commerce with Germans: the German *posits as equal* . . . If I subtract my commerce with a few artists, above all with Richard Wagner, I have experienced not a single good hour with Germans . . . Supposing the profoundest spirit of all the millennia appeared among the Germans, some goose of the Capitol would opine that its very unbeautiful soul came at least equally into consideration . . . I cannot endure this race, with which one is always in bad company, which has no finger for *nuances* – woe is me! I am a *nuance* – which has no *esprit* in its feet and cannot even walk ... In the end the Germans have no idea whatever how common they are; but that is the superlative of commonness – they are not even *ashamed* of being mere Germans ... They feel free to discuss everything, they even consider themselves decisive, I fear they have even decided about me ... My whole life is the proof *de rigueur* of these propositions. I seek in it in vain for a single sign of tact, of *délicatesse* towards me. From Jews yes, never yet from Germans. My nature directs that I am mild and benevolent towards everyone – I have a *right* not to make distinctions –: this does not prevent me from keeping my eyes open. I except no one, least of all my friends – I hope in the end that this has not diminished my humanity towards them! There are five or six things which have always been a point of honour with me. – It remains none the less true that almost every letter which has reached me for years past strikes me as a piece of cynicism: there is more cynicism in benevolence towards me than in any kind of hatred ... I tell each of my friends to his face that he never thinks it worth the trouble to *study* any of my writings: I divine from the smallest of signs that they do not even know what is in them. As for my Zarathustra, who of my friends would have seen more in it than an impermissible piece of presumption but one that was fortunately a matter of complete indifference? ... Ten years: and no one in Germany has made it a question of conscience to defend my name against the absurd silence under which it has lain buried: it was a foreigner, a Dane, who was the first to possess sufficient refinement of instinct *and courage* for that, who inveighed against my supposed friends ... At which German university today would lectures on my philosophy be possible such as were given last spring by Dr Georg Brandes in Copenhagen – who therewith once more proved himself a psychologist? – I myself have never suffered from any of this; I am not injured by what is *necessary*; *amor fati* is my innermost nature. This does not mean, however, that I do not enjoy the irony, even the world-historic irony. And so, about two years before the shattering thunder-clap of the *Revaluation* which will set the earth into convulsions, I sent the 'Wagner Case' into the world: my notion was that the Germans should once more blunder immortally about me and so *eternalize* themselves! there was just about enough time left! – Was that achieved? – Charmingly, my Herr– Teutons! I compliment you . . .

WHY I AM A DESTINY

I KNOW my fate. One day there will be associated with my name the recollection of something frightful – of a crisis like no other before on earth, of the profoundest collision of conscience, of a decision evoked *against* everything that until then had been believed in, demanded, sanctified. I am not a man, I am dynamite. – And with all that there is nothing in me of a founder of a religion – religions are affairs of the rabble, I have need of washing my hands after contact with religious people ... I do not *want* 'believers', I think I am too malicious to believe in myself, I never speak to masses ... I have a terrible fear I shall one day be pronounced *holy*: one will guess why I bring out this book *beforehand*; it is intended to prevent people from making mischief with me ... I do not want to be a saint, rather even a buffoon ... Perhaps I am a buffoon ... And none the less, or rather *not* none the less – for there has hitherto been nothing more mendacious than saints – the truth speaks out of me. – But my truth is *dreadful*: for hitherto the *lie* has been called truth. – *Revaluation of all values*: this is my formula for an act of supreme coming-to-oneself on the part of mankind which in me has become flesh and genius. It is my fate to have to be the first *decent* human being, to know myself in opposition to the mendaciousness of millennia ... I was the first to *discover* the truth, in that I was the first to sense – *smell* – the lie as lie ... My genius is in my nostrils ... I contradict as has never been contradicted and am none the less the opposite of a negative spirit. I am a *bringer of good tidings* such as there has never been, I know tasks from such a height that any conception of them has hitherto been lacking; only after me is it possible to hope again. With all that I am necessarily a man of fatality. For when truth steps into battle with the lie of millennia we shall have convulsions, an earthquake spasm, a transposition of valley and mountain such as has never been dreamed of. The concept politics has then become completely absorbed into a war of spirits, all the power-structures of the old society have been blown into the air – they one and all reposed on the lie: there will be wars such as there have never yet been on earth. Only after me will there be *grand politics* on earth.

2

Does one want a formula for a destiny *that has become man*? It stands in my Zarathustra.

– and he who wants to be a creator in good and evil has first to be a destroyer and break values.
   Thus the greatest evil belongs with the greatest good: this, however, is the creative good.

I am by far the most terrible human being there has ever been; this does not mean I shall not be the most beneficent. I know joy in *destruction* to a degree corresponding to my *strength* for destruction – in both I obey my dionysian nature, which does not know how to separate No-doing from Yes-saying. I am the first *immoralist*: I am therewith the *destroyer par excellence.* –

3

I have not been asked, as I should have been asked, what the name Zarathustra means in precisely my mouth, in the mouth of the first immoralist: for what constitutes the tremendous uniqueness of that Persian in history is precisely the opposite of this. Zarathustra was the first to see in the struggle between good and evil the actual wheel in the working of things: the translation of morality into the realm of metaphysics, as force, cause, end-in-itself, is *his* work. But this question is itself at bottom its own answer. Zarathustra *created* this most fateful of errors, morality: consequently he must also be the first to *recognize* it. Not only has he had longer and greater experience here than any other thinker – the whole of history is indeed the experimental refutation of the proposition of a so-called 'moral world-order' –: what is more important is that Zarathustra is more truthful than any other thinker. His teaching, and his alone, upholds truthfulness as the supreme virtue – that is to say, the opposite of the *cowardice* of the 'idealist', who takes flight in face of reality; Zarathustra has more courage in him than all other thinkers put together. To tell the truth and *to shoot well with arrows*: that is Persian virtue. – Have I been understood? The self-overcoming of morality through truthfulness, the self-overcoming of the moralist into his opposite – *into me* – that is what the name Zarathustra means in my mouth.

4

At bottom my expression *immoralist* involves two denials. I deny first a type of man who has hitherto counted as the highest, the *good*, the *benevolent*, *beneficent*; I deny secondly a kind of morality which has come to be accepted and to dominate as morality in itself – *décadence* morality, in more palpable terms *Christian* morality. The second contradiction might be seen as the decisive one, since the over-valuation of goodness and benevolence by and large already counts with me as a consequence of *décadence*, as a symptom of weakness, as incompatible with an ascending and affirmative life: denial *and destruction* is a condition of affirmation. – I deal first of all with the psychology of the good man. In order to assess what a type of man is worth one has to compute how much his preservation costs – one has to know the conditions of his existence. The condition for the existence of the good is the *lie* –: expressed differently, the *desire* not to see at any price what is the fundamental constitution of reality, that is to say *not* such as to call forth benevolent instincts at all times, even less such as to permit at all times an interference by short-sighted good-natured hands. To regard *states of distress* in general as an objection, as something that must be *abolished*, is the *niaiserie par excellence*, in a general sense a real disaster in its consequences, a fatality of stupidity – almost as stupid as would be the will to abolish bad weather – perhaps from pity to the poor ... In the general economy of the whole the fearfulnesses of reality (in the affects, in the desires, in the will to power) are to an incalculable degree more necessary than any form of petty happiness, so-called 'goodness'; since the latter is conditioned by falsity of instinct one must even be cautious about granting it a place at all. I shall have a grand occasion of demonstrating the measurelessly uncanny consequences for the whole of history of *optimism*, that offspring of the *homines optimi*. Zarathustra, the first to grasp that optimism is just as *décadent* as pessimism and perhaps more harmful, says: *good men never tell the truth. The good taught you false shores and false securities: you were born and kept in the lies of the good. Everything has been distorted and twisted down to its very bottom through the good.* Fortunately the world has not been constructed for the satisfaction of instincts such as would permit merely good-natured herd animals to find their narrow happiness in it; to demand that everything should become 'good man', herd animal, blue-eyed, benevolent, 'beautiful soul' – or, as Mr Herbert Spencer wants, altruistic, would mean to deprive existence of its *great* character, would mean to castrate mankind and to reduce it to a paltry Chinadom. – *And this has been attempted!* ... *Precisely this has been called morality* ... In this sense Zarathustra calls the good now 'the last men', now the 'beginning of the end'; above all he feels them to be the *most harmful species of man*, because they preserve their existence as much at the expense of *truth* as at the expense of the *future*.

The good – cannot *create*, they are always the beginning of the end –

– they crucify him who writes *new* values on new law-tables, they sacrifice the future *to themselves*, they crucify the whole human future!

The good – have always been the beginning of the end . . .

And whatever harm the world-calumniators may do, *the harm the good do is the most harmful harm.*

5

Zarathustra, the first psychologist of the good, is – consequently – a friend of the wicked. When a *décadence*-species of man has risen to the rank of the highest species of man, this can happen only at the expense of its antithetical species, the species of man strong and certain of life. When the herd-animal is resplendent in the glow of the highest virtue, the exceptional man must be devalued to the wicked man. When mendaciousness at any price appropriates the word 'truth' for its perspective, what is actually veracious must be discovered bearing the worst names. Zarathustra here leaves no doubt: he says that it was knowledge of precisely the good, the 'best', which made him feel horror at man in general; it was out of *this* repugnance that the wings grew which 'carried him to distant futures' – he does not dissemble that it is precisely in relation to the *good* that *his* type of man, a relatively superhuman type, is superhuman, that the good and just would call his superman a *devil* . . .

You highest men my eyes have encountered! This is my doubt of you and my secret laughter: I think you would call my superman – a devil!

Your souls are so unfamiliar with what is great that the superman would be *fearful* to you in his *goodness* . . .

It is at this point and nowhere else that one must make a start if one is to understand what Zarathustra's intentions are: the species of man he delineates delineates reality *as it is*: he is strong enough for it – he is not estranged from or entranced by it, he is *reality itself*, he still has all that is fearful and questionable in reality in him, *only thus can man possess greatness* . . .

6

— But there is also another sense in which I have chosen for myself the word *immoralist* as a mark of distinction and badge of honour; I am proud to possess this word which sets me off against the whole of humanity. No one has yet felt *Christian* morality as *beneath* him: that requires a height, a farsightedness, a hitherto altogether unheard-of psychological profundity and abysmalness. Christian morality has hitherto been the Circe of all thinkers — they stood in its service. — Who before me has entered the caverns out of which the poisonous blight of this kind of ideal — *world-calumny!* — wells up? Who has even ventured to suspect *that* these caverns exist? Who before me at all among philosophers has been a *psychologist* and not rather its opposite 'higher swindler', 'idealist'? Before me there was no psychology. — To be the first here can be a curse, it is in any case a destiny: *for one is also the first to despise* . . . *Disgust* at mankind is my danger . . .

7

Have I been understood? — What defines me, what sets me apart from all the rest of mankind, is that I have *unmasked* Christian morality. That is why I needed a word which would embody the sense of a challenge to everyone. Not to have opened its eyes here sooner counts to me as the greatest piece of uncleanliness which humanity has on its conscience, as self-deception become instinct, as a fundamental will *not* to observe every event, every cause, every reality, as false-coinage *in psychologicis* to the point of crime. Blindness in the face of Christianity is the *crime par excellence* — the crime *against life* . . . The millennia, the peoples, the first and the last, the philosophers and the old women — except for five or six moments of history, me as the seventh – on this point they are all worthy of one another. The Christian has hitherto been *the* 'moral being', a curiosity without equal – and, *as* 'moral being', more absurd, mendacious, vain, frivolous, *harmful to himself* than even the greatest despiser of mankind could have allowed himself to dream. Christian morality – the most malicious form of the will to the lie, the actual Circe of mankind: that which has *ruined* it. It is *not* error as error which horrifies me at the sight of this, *not* the millennia-long lack of 'good will', of discipline, of decency, of courage in spiritual affairs which betrays itself in its victory – it is the lack of nature, it is the utterly ghastly fact that *anti-nature* itself has received the highest honours as morality, and has hung over mankind as law, as categorical imperative! . . . To blunder to this extent, *not* as an individual, *not* as a people, but as mankind! . . . That contempt has been taught for the primary instincts of life; that a 'soul', a 'spirit' has been *lyingly invented* in order to destroy the body; that one teaches that there is something unclean in the precondition of life, sexuality; that the evil principle is sought in that which is most profoundly necessary for prosperity, in *strict* selfishness (– the very word is slanderous!); that on the other hand one sees in the typical signs of decline and contradictoriness of instinct, in the 'selfless', in loss of centre of gravity, in 'depersonalization' and 'love of one's neighbour' (– *lust for* one's neighbour!) the *higher* value, what am I saying! *value in itself*! . . . *What*! could mankind itself be in *décadence*? has it always been? – What is certain is that it has been *taught* only *décadence* values as supreme values. The morality of unselfing is the morality of decline *par excellence*, the fact 'I am perishing' translated into the imperative 'you all *shall* perish' – and *not only* into the imperative! . . . This sole morality which has hitherto been taught, the morality of unselfing, betrays a will to the end, it *denies* the very foundations of life. – Let us here leave the possibility open that it is not mankind which is degenerating but only that parasitic species of man the *priest*, who with the aid of morality has lied himself up to being the determiner of mankind's values – who divines in Christian morality his means to *power* ... And that is in fact *my* insight: the teachers, the leaders of mankind, theologians included, have also one and all been *décadents*: *thence* the revaluation of all values into the inimical to life, *thence* morality ... *Definition of morality*: morality – the idiosyncrasy of *décadents* with the hidden intention of *avenging themselves on life – and* successfully. I set store by *this* definition. –

8

– Have I been understood? – I have not just now said a word that I could not have said five years ago through the mouth of Zarathustra. – The *unmasking* of Christian morality is an event without equal, a real catastrophe. He who exposes it is a *force majeure*, a destiny – he breaks the history of mankind into two parts. One lives *before* him, one lives *after* him ... The lightning-bolt of truth struck precisely that which formerly stood highest: he who grasps *what* was then destroyed had better see whether he has anything at all left in his hands. Everything hitherto called 'truth' is recognized as the most harmful, malicious, most subterranean form of the lie; the holy pretext of 'improving' mankind as the cunning to *suck out* life itself and to make it anaemic. Morality as *vampirism* ... He who unmasks morality has therewith unmasked the valuelessness of all values which are or have been believed in; he no longer sees in the most revered, even *canonized* types of man anything venerable, he sees in them the most fateful kind of abortion, fateful *because they exercise fascination* ... The concept 'God' invented as the antithetical concept to life – everything harmful, noxious, slanderous, the whole mortal enmity against life brought into one terrible unity! The concept 'the Beyond', 'real world' invented so as to deprive of value the *only* world which exists – so as to leave over no goal, no reason, no task for our earthly reality! The concept 'soul', 'spirit', finally even 'immortal soul', invented so as to despise the body, so as to make it sick – 'holy' – so as to bring to all the things in life which deserve serious attention, the questions of nutriment, residence, cleanliness, weather, a horrifying frivolity! Instead of health 'salvation of the soul' – which is to say a *folie circulaire* between spasms of atonement and redemption hysteria! The concept 'sin' invented together with the instrument of torture which goes with it, the concept of 'free will', so as to confuse the instincts, so as to make mistrust of the instincts into second nature! In the concept of the 'selfless', of the 'self-denying' the actual badge of *décadence*, being *lured* by the harmful, no longer being *able* to discover where one's advantage lies, self-destruction, made the sign of value in general, made 'duty', 'holiness', the 'divine' in man! Finally – it is the most fearful – in the concept of the *good* man common cause made with everything weak, sick, ill-constructed, suffering from itself, all that *which ought to perish* – the law of *selection* crossed, an ideal made of opposition to the proud and well-constituted, to the affirmative man, to the man certain of the future and guaranteeing the future – the latter is henceforth called the *evil man* ... And all this was believed in *as morality*! – *Ecrasez l'infâme!* –

9

– Have I been understood? – *Dionysos against the Crucified* ...

NOTES

FOREWORD

1. *heaviest demand.* The forthcoming *Revaluation of all Values* – together with the effect it may be expected to produce – is presumably what is meant.

3. Nitimur in *vetitum.* We strive after the forbidden (Ovid).

4. '*It is the stillest . . . guide the world*'. Quoted from *Thus Spoke Zarathustra*, Part Two: 'The Stillest Hour'.

The figs are falling . . . sky and afternoon. Quoted from *Zarathustra*, Part Two: 'On the Blissful Islands'.

décadent. Nietzsche employs, here and elsewhere, the French word, since none with precisely this meaning was available to him in German.

I now go away . . . will I return to you. Quoted from *Zarathustra*, Part One: 'Of the Bestowing Virtue'.

'On This Perfect Day . . .'

first book of the Revaluation of all Values. Nietzsche was at the date of *Ecce Homo* still referring to the just completed *Anti-Christ* as the first book of the forthcoming *Revaluation*. Either immediately before or immediately after the mental breakdown of 3 January 1889 he withdrew this designation by erasing it from the title-page of the manuscript.

Songs of Zarathustra: i.e. the *Dionysos-Dithyramben*, published in 1892.

Why I am So Wise

2. *as* summa summarum: as a totality.

3. *I am a pure-blooded Polish nobleman.* This seems to have been a 'family legend' which Nietzsche's hatred of the *Reich* inspired him to

propagate during his last sane years; but it is refuted by the genealogical evidence. Nietzsche's ancestry has been traced back to the sixteenth century and over two hundred ancestors are known: all are German, and the name Nietzsche is, together with its cognate forms (e.g. Nitsche, Nitzke), a common one in central Germany.

At the end of December 1888 Nietzsche posted to his publisher a set of corrections to the manuscript of *Ecce Homo*. The revised section 3 was discovered among the papers of Peter Gast in the Nietzsche collection of the Goethe-Schiller Archive in Weimar in 1969. Gast had sent the manuscript of this section to Nietzsche's mother and sister, who destroyed it; but he had copied it out. This is the first edition of *Ecce Homo* in English to include it. The passage reproduced below is the original section 3 published in the first edition, and all subsequent English translations.

This twofold succession of experiences, this accessibility to me of apparently separate worlds, is repeated in my nature in every respect – I am a *Doppelgänger*, I have a 'second' face in addition to the first one. *And* perhaps also a third ... Even by virtue of my descent I am permitted to look beyond all merely locally, merely nationally conditioned perspectives, it costs me no effort to be a 'good European'. On the other hand I am perhaps more German than present-day Germans, mere Reich Germans, are still capable of being – I the last *anti-political* German. And yet my ancestors were Polish noblemen: I have preserved from them much racial instinct, who knows? ultimately even the *liberum veto*. When I consider how often I am addressed as a Pole and by Poles themselves, how rarely I am taken for a German, it might appear that German has only been *sprinkled on* to me. But my mother, Franziska Oehler, is in any event something very German; likewise my paternal grandmother, Erdmuthe Krause. The latter lived her entire youth in the middle of good old Weimar, not without coming into contact with Goethe's circle. Her brother, Professor of Theology Krause of Königsberg, was called to Weimar as general superintendent after Herder's death. It is not impossible that her mother, my great-grandmother, appears in the young Goethe's diary under the name 'Muthgen'. Her second marriage was with the superintendent Nietzsche of Eilenburg; it was on the day of the great war year 1813 on which Napoleon entered Eilenburg with his general staff, on 10 October, that she had her confinement. As a Saxon she was a great admirer of Napoleon; it could be that I am so still. My father born 1813, died 1849. Before he took over the pastorship of the parish of Röcken, not far from Lützen, he lived for some years in the castle of Altenburg and instructed the four princesses there. His pupils are the Queen of Hanover, Grand-Duchess Constantin, the Grand-Duchess of Oldenburg and Princess Therese of Saxe-Altenburg. He was full of a deep reverence for King Friedrich Wilhelm the Fourth of Prussia, from whom he also received his pastorship; the events of 1848 distressed him beyond measure. I myself, born on the birthday of the said king, on 15 October, received as was appropriate the Hohenzollern names *Friedrich* Wilhelm. The choice of this day had at any rate one advantage: throughout my entire childhood my birthday was a holiday. – I regard it as a great privilege to have had such a father: it even seems to me that whatever else of privileges I possess is thereby explained – life, the great Yes to life, *not* included. Above all that it requires no intention on my part, but only a mere waiting, for me to enter involuntarily into a world of exalted and delicate things: I am at home there, my innermost passion becomes free only there. That I paid for this privilege almost with my life is certainly no unfair trade. – To understand anything at all of my Zarathustra one has perhaps to possess a qualification similar to that which I possess – to have one foot *beyond* life . . .

'*good European*': a coinage of Nietzsche's, probably as an antithesis to 'good German'.

liberum veto: the right to veto legislation possessed by the nobility of the Polish Diet.

the events of 1848: the revolutionary outbreaks in many parts of Europe which characterized this year.

4. *Heinrich von Stein*. He had been tutor to Wagner's son, Siegfried, and Wagner's last published writing was an introduction to his book *Helden und Welt* (1883). He died in 1887, at the age of thirty.

swamp of Dühring: Eugen Dühring (1833–1901), philosopher and economist. The 'swamp' is probably anti-Semitism.

'*Zarathustra's Temptation*': Part Four of *Thus Spoke Zarathustra* is meant.

6. *ressentiment*. French in the original, for a similar reason to the author's employment of *décadent*.

8. *pure folly*. A favourite joke of Nietzsche's, here not very apposite. (I quote the note on it from my translation of *Twilight of the Idols*: Parsifal, eponymous hero of Wagner's last opera, is described as a pure, i.e. chaste, fool [*reine Tor*] whose naivety is proof against temptation of every kind. Nietzsche considered the plot of *Parsifal* preposterous and persistently uses the phrase '*reine Torheit*' [pure folly] in the sense of *complete folly*.)

Yet what happened . . . against the wind. Quoted, with slight alteration, from *Zarathustra*, Part Two: 'Of the Rabble'.

Why I am So Clever

1. (*It is said . . . in this domain*): due, presumably, to the occupation of Saxony by Prussia during the German War of 1866.

alla tedesca: in the German fashion.

Piedmont: the Italian province of which Turin, where *Ecce Homo* was written, is the chief city.

Assiduity . . . holy spirit. Quoted from *Twilight of the Idols*.

3. *Frau Cosima Wagner*, born Liszt, Wagner's second wife and (by the date of *Ecce Homo*) widow.

ex ungue Napoleonem: from the claw, Napoleon (from *ex ungue leonum* = from the claw [you can reconstruct or infer] the lion).

4. *mere Germans*: Heine was a Jew, Nietzsche supposed himself descended from Poles (see note above).

American shallow-pates and muddle-heads. Alludes to the American origin of the Baconian movement, with the implication that Nietzsche does not derive his own views from it.

9. *nosce te ipsum*: know thyself.

10. *amor fati*: love of (one's) fate.

Why I Write Such Good Books

1. '*non legor, non legar*': I am not read, I will not be read.

Dr V. Widmann (1842–1911), minor Swiss poet.

Karl Spitteler (1845–1924), major Swiss writer, Nobel Prize-winner for literature in 1919.

'*Kreuzzeitung*': an extreme reactionary newspaper.

3. '*beautiful souls*': phrase from Goethe's *Wilhelm Meisters Lehrjahre*.

To you . . . hate to calculate. Quoted from *Zarathustra*, Part Three: 'Of the Vision and the Riddle'.

5. *eternal-womanly*: from the concluding chorus of Goethe's *Faust*.

The Birth of Tragedy

1. *battle of Wörth . . . walls of Metz*: i.e. during service in the Franco-Prussian War of 1870.

The Untimely Essays

2. *'old faith and new'*: the title of the book by David Strauss, an assault on which is the starting point of the first *Untimely Meditation*.
'Berlin blue': i.e. Prussian blue.
Ewald of Göttingen: Heinrich Ewald (1803–75), theologian.
Bruno Bauer (1809–82), theologian.
Professor Hoffmann of Würzburg: Franz Hoffmann (1804–81), writer on philosophy.
Karl Hillebrand (1829–84), historian and essayist.

Human, All Too Human

2. *the late Brendel*: Franz Brendel (1811–68), writer on music and a Wagnerian.
Bayreuther Blätter: the magazine, founded in 1878, of the Wagnerian faction.
Nohl, Pohl, Kohl. Ludwig Nohl and Richard Pohl were writers on music and Wagnerians; *Kohl* means 'cabbage', colloquially 'nonsense'.
6. *But what is the main . . . all great perceptions*. Quoted, with slight alterations and easily identifiable interpolations, from *Human, All Too Human*, section 37.

Thus Spoke Zarathustra

1. *that sacred hour . . . died in Venice*. If this is to be taken literally, it means at 3.30 p.m. on 13 February 1883.
2. *the clock-hand . . . the tragedy* begins: alludes to and inverts the stopping of the clock at midnight at the *end* of Faust's tragedy.
3. *'here all things . . . speech from you –'*. Quoted, with slight alterations, from *Zarathustra*, Part Three: 'The Home-Coming'.
4. *Aquila*: originally a fortress, established by Konradin, son of

Friedrich the Second, during the thirteenth-century conflict between the papacy and the Hohenstaufen dynasty.

palazzo del Quirinale: then the official residence of the king.

third and last. Part Four was at the date of *Ecce Homo* still unpublished.

6. *I form circles . . . holier mountains.* Quoted from *Zarathustra*, Part Three: 'Of Old and New Law-Tables'.

the soul which possesses . . . ebb and flow. Quoted from the same source.

7. *before sunrise*: title of a 'dithyrambic' chapter of *Zarathustra*, Part Three.

8. *I walk among men . . . I call redemption.* Quoted from *Zarathustra*, Part Two: 'Of Redemption'.

no more to will . . . gods to me now! Quoted from *Zarathustra*, Part Two: 'On the Blissful Islands'.

Genealogy of Morals

'*For man will . . . than not will*'. Quoted from *On the Genealogy of Morals*, Third Essay: 'What is the Meaning of Ascetic Ideals?'

Twilight of the Idols

2. '*obscure impulse*' . . . *the right path*: alludes to the lines 'Ein guter Mensch in seinem dunklen Drange/Ist sich des rechten Weges wohl bewusst' (A good man is, in his obscure impulse, well aware of the right path), spoken by the Lord in the prologue to Goethe's *Faust*.

3. *I attacked the tremendous task . . . banks of the Po.* This passage records the writing, between 3 and 30 September 1888, of *The Anti-Christ*.

Claude Lorrain (1600–82), painter.

The Wagner Case

Written before *Twilight*: the chronological order has, in this one instance, been departed from, probably so as to conclude the chapter with Wagner and the Germans.

1. *ridendo dicere* severum: laughing to say what is serious – the motto of *The Wagner Case*.

old artillerist: alludes to his one-year's military service in 1867–8.

the Trumpeter of Säckingen: a poem by Joseph Viktor von Scheffel (1853) which enjoyed in Germany the same order of popularity as Browning's *The Pied Piper of Hamelin* did in England; but Nietzsche may perhaps be referring to Viktor Nessler's opera based on it (1884), which was also very successful.

cunning: *listiger*, a pun on Liszt.

2. *Vischer*: Ernst Theodor Vischer (1807–87), aesthetician.

Why I am a Destiny

2. *and he who wants to be . . . the creative good*. Quoted, with slight alterations, from *Zarathustra*, Part Two: 'Of Self-Overcoming'.

3. *Zarathustra*. The historical Zarathustra (*Greek* Zoroastres), after whom Nietzsche named the central figure of *Thus Spoke Zarathustra*, is the founder of the Persian religion called in English Zoroastrianism. He is thought to have lived in the seventh century BC.

4. *good men never . . . through the good*. Quoted from *Zarathustra*, Part Three: 'Of Old and New Law-Tables'.

The good . . . most harmful harm: from the same source.

5. *You highest men . . . in his goodness*. Quoted from *Zarathustra*, Part Two: 'Of Manly Prudence'.

8. *Ecrasez l'infâme*: crush the infamous thing! (Voltaire, with reference to the church).

READ MORE IN PENGUIN

In every corner of the world, on every subject under the sun, Penguin represents quality and variety – the very best in publishing today.

For complete information about books available from Penguin – including Puffins, Penguin Classics and Arkana – and how to order them, write to us at the appropriate address below. Please note that for copyright reasons the selection of books varies from country to country.

In the United Kingdom: Please write to *Dept. JC, Penguin Books Ltd, FREEPOST, West Drayton, Middlesex UB7 0BR*

If you have any difficulty in obtaining a title, please send your order with the correct money, plus ten per cent for postage and packaging, to *PO Box No. 11, West Drayton, Middlesex UB7 0BR*

In the United States: Please write to *Penguin USA Inc., 375 Hudson Street, New York, NY 10014*

In Canada: Please write to *Penguin Books Canada Ltd, 10 Alcorn Avenue, Suite 300, Toronto, Ontario M4V 3B2*

In Australia: Please write to *Penguin Books Australia Ltd, 487 Maroondah Highway, Ringwood, Victoria 3134*

In New Zealand: Please write to *Penguin Books (NZ) Ltd, 182–190 Wairau Road, Private Bag, Takapuna, Auckland 9*

In India: Please write to *Penguin Books India Pvt Ltd, 706 Eros Apartments, 56 Nehru Place, New Delhi 110 019*

In the Netherlands: Please write to *Penguin Books Netherlands B.V., Keizersgracht 231 NL–1016 DV Amsterdam*

In Germany: Please write to *Penguin Books Deutschland GmbH, Friedrichstrasse 10–12, W–6000 Frankfurt/Main 1*

In Spain: Please write to *Penguin Books S. A., C. San Bernardo 117–6° E–28015 Madrid*

In Italy: Please write to *Penguin Italia s.r.l., Via Felice Casati 20, I–20124 Milano*

In France: Please write to *Penguin France S. A., 17 rue Lejeune, F–31000 Toulouse*

In Japan: Please write to *Penguin Books Japan, Ishikiribashi Building, 2–5–4, Suido, Tokyo 112*

In Greece: Please write to *Penguin Hellas Ltd, Dimocritou 3, GR–106 71 Athens*

In South Africa: Please write to *Longman Penguin Southern Africa (Pty) Ltd, Private Bag X08, Bertsham 2013*